OCEAN
AND SEA

OCE
AND SEA

EAN

STEVE PARKER
with
THE CENSUS OF MARINE LIFE

SCHOLASTIC discover more™

How to discover mor

This book is simple to use and enjoy, but knowing a little bit about how it works will help you discover more about oceans and seas. Have a great read!

How the pages work
The book is divided into chapters, such as **Life in the ocean**. Each chapter is made up of stand-alone spreads (double pages) that focus on specific topics.

The environment
The oceans are a huge but endangered part of our world. The last section of this book (pages 94–107) explores these dangers and shows how you can help.

Spread heading
The title of the spread lets you know what the subject is.

Fantastic facts
BIG text gives an amazing fact or quote!

Introduction
Most spreads have a general introduction to the subject.

Fact boxes
Some spreads include a fact box for quick information and comparison.

Identity labels
Many pictures have labels to tell you exactly what they are.

Threatened species [Help!]

Right now, in all the world's oceans, creatures are at risk of becoming extinct (dying out forever). Many people are unaware of the huge problems, partly because sea animals and the dangers they face are hidden beneath the waves. Threats vary greatly, from pollution and global warming to being caught accidentally in fishing nets or on purpose for our dinner tables.

How threatened?
For each species, experts need information: How many are there? How widely are they spread? How fast do they breed? They also need to know the dangers they face, such as loss of food or habitats.

Vulnerable
In this group are animals that are not in immediate danger— but they could be in coming years. We need to take early action to protect them and their habitats.

Endangered
These animals are already in serious trouble. Without our urgent help, their numbers will continue to fall until they no longer exist.

Critically endangered
Creatures in this most serious category are staring extinction in the face. Without drastic action now, they will not make it. They could be gone in 30 years or even sooner.

Until the 1980s, sperm whale Whales died so

MANATEE   POLAR BEAR

GALÁPAGOS FUR SEAL   BLUE WHALE

WESTERN GRAY WHALE

LEATHERBACK TURTLE   SMALLTOOTH SAWFISH

Threats from humans

Beluga whale	Pollution, boat disturbance, hunting in some areas
Blue whale	Boat strikes, tangling in fishing gear
Humpback whale	Boat strikes, illegal hunting
Killer whale	Loss of food, pollution, oil spills, boat disturbance
Spotted seal	Melting sea ice, hunting for skins
Leatherback turtle	Disturbed nests, pollution, eating floating garbage
Loggerhead turtle	Tangling in fishing gear
Sockeye salmon	Bycatch, changing ocean currents
Rockeye salmon	Diseases from salmon farms
Black abalone	Overfishing, disease due to global warming
Elkhorn coral	Diseases made worse by warming waters
Staghorn coral	As above, also water clouded with sediments

Digital companion book

Download your free, all-new digital book:

Shark Spotter

Log on to
www.scholastic.com/ discovermore

Enter your unique code:
RXC2RPRHJFXW

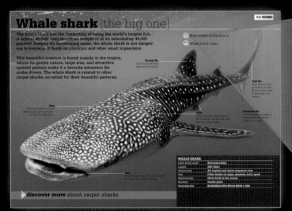

Whale shark [the big one]

The whale shark has the distinction of being the world's largest fish. A typical 40-foot-long specimen weighs in at an astounding 45,000 pounds! Despite its threatening name, the whale shark is not dangerous to humans. It feeds on plankton and other small organisms.

This beautiful creature is found mainly in the tropics, where its gentle nature, large size, and attractive spotted pattern make it a favorite attraction for scuba divers. The whale shark is related to other carpet sharks, so-called for their beautiful patterns.

discover more about carpet sharks

Meet every kind of shark up close.

Carpet sharks [patter

The whale shark is the largest of 30 species of sharks known as carpet sharks. They all have patterned and mottled skin that looks like a carpet design! Carpet sharks are often large, but rarely dangerous to humans. Some bear live young, others lay eggs. Many species are bottom feeders, primarily eating mollusks and crustaceans. Most have barbels, whiskerlike organs that house taste buds and are used to search for

Wobbegong

Click the pop-ups for essential shark facts.

Spread types

Look out for different kinds of spreads such as stats spreads and history spreads. There are others, too—that's what makes the book so interesting.

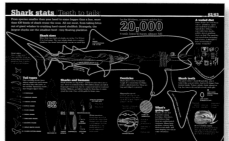

STATS SPREAD

A stats spread is packed full of facts, amazing statistics, and fun infographics.

Pirates | 84/85

HISTORY SPREAD

A timeline column gives you the most important dates and events in the history of a topic.

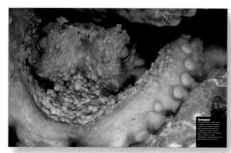

Octopus

PHOTOGRAPHIC SPREAD

This type of spread focuses on an extraordinary subject, often providing an unfamiliar view, such as this sleepy octopus in its seabed home.

More here columns

This feature suggests books to read, places and websites to visit, and things to do and not do.

GALAPAGOS MARINE IGUANA

GREEN TURTLE

PACIFIC RAY

BLUEFIN TUNA

*..., a secretion in
...ed in scents.
...uld smell good!*

100/101

OCEANS UNDER THREAT

More here

📖 *Miss L'eau* by Theresa Katz

🖱 **IUCN Red Lists**
Census of Marine Life
endangered habitat loss
survival **overfishing**

✓ Support beaches where marine conservation is a priority. "Adopt" a marine animal through a good program. Join an underwater cleanup group. If you go boating, watch out for marine life.

❗ Don't buy seafood, such as tuna and shrimp, unless it is fished in a responsible way.

🔍 **bycatch:** animals caught accidentally, such as turtles, dolphins, or sharks trapped in nets intended for shoals of small fish.

Ⓦ **sustainable:** able to be maintained at a certain level, such as fish being caught in numbers that allow them to reproduce and grow.

Key to symbols in **More here** columns

📖 *Suggested reading*

🖱 *Keywords for web searches*

✓ *Do*

❗ *Don't do*

▭ *Watch online*

➦ *Places to visit*

🔍 *Mini-glossary*

Ⓦ *Hot words*

Mini-glossary

This explains challenging words and phrases found on the spread.

Hot words

These words aren't on the spread, but they relate to the topic.

Glossary and index

The glossary explains words and phrases that might not be explained fully on the spread or in the **More here** column. The index can help you find pages throughout the book on which words and topics appear.

Fish

Fish are water animals (aquatic) that are usually born from eggs and breathe through gills. They are vertebrates, that is, animals with a backbone and an internal skeleton. It is hard to determine exactly how many different species, or kinds, of fish there are. We know of more than 21,000 different species of fish today. This means that there are more species of fish than all the other vertebrate species combined. New species of fish are constantly being discovered as the deep sea and other remote waters are explored, leading scientists to speculate that the actual number may be closer to 28,000 species.

Fish are usually divided into three major groups: the primitive jawless fishes, including lampreys and hagfishes; and two groups of jawed fishes—the cartilaginous fishes, including sharks, skates, and rays, and the bony fishes, which are by far the largest group and include most of the familiar fishes such as trout, perch, bass, cod, halibut, and tropical fishes raised in home aquaria. Despite their name, shellfish, of course, are not fish at all; these invertebrate animals are either crustaceans (such as shrimp, lobsters) or mollusks (such as clams, oysters).

500 million years
that's the incredible length of time that fish have been on Earth!

Read in-depth shark and ocean encyclopedia entries.

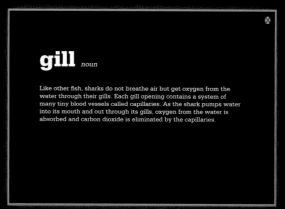

gill *noun*

Like other fish, sharks do not breathe air but get oxygen from the water through their gills. Each gill opening contains a system of many tiny blood vessels called capillaries. As the shark pumps water into its mouth and out through its gills, oxygen from the water is absorbed and carbon dioxide is eliminated by the capillaries.

Look up shark and ocean words.

Consultant: Darlene Trew Crist, Director of Communications, Census of Marine Life

Literacy consultant: Jane E. Mekkelsen, Literacy & Learning Connections LLC

Project editor: Gill Denton

Project art editor: Miranda Brown

Editor: Susan McKeever

US editors: Elizabeth Hester, Beth Sutinis

Art director: Bryn Walls

Managing editor: Miranda Smith

Cover designer: Natalie Godwin

DTP: John Goldsmid

Visual content editor: Diane Allford-Trotman

Executive Director of Photography, Scholastic: Steve Diamond

"The sea, once it casts its spell, holds one in its net of wonder forever."

—JACQUES YVES COUSTEAU

Library of Congress Cataloging-in-Publication Data Available

ISBN 978-0-545-33022-0

10 9 8 7 6 5 4 3 2 1   12 13 14 15 16

Printed in Singapore   46
First edition, January 2012

Scholastic is constantly working to lessen the environmental impact of our manufacturing processes. To view our industry-leading paper procurement policy, visit www.scholastic.com/paperpolicy.

Contents

Antarctic tours

The icy waters of the Southern Ocean surrounding Antarctica have become a popular vacation destination. It is possible to visit only during the Antarctic summer, between November and March, because in winter, the buildup of sea ice could trap a ship.

Delicate drifter

Oceans teem with startling and
unfamiliar life. This fragile, frilly
medusa (a fully grown jellyfish,
Desmonema glaciale) lives near
the surface in freezing Antarctic
waters. Its "bell" can grow
to more than 3.3 feet
(1 m) wide.

All a
oce

When did the world have only one ocean?

* How does the Moon pull oceans onto the land?

Why does an ocean have shelves?

bout

ans

Ocean waters [Top down]

We walk around on solid ground, yet 71 percent of Earth is covered by water. From rock pools to mighty oceans, these waters are home to a huge variety of plants and animals. Over millions of years, they have adapted to these often hostile saltwater habitats.

Sea salts
The salt in seawater is sodium chloride (table salt). It's not good for most sea creatures, so internal chemical pumps in the animals' bodies work constantly to remove it.

Seeing in the sea

Sunlight is made up of all the colors in the rainbow, but each color fades at a different rate with depth. Red gets fainter fastest, then orange, and so on. So the deeper you dive, the bluer—and darker—it becomes. Many animal eyes are adapted to detect blue light best.

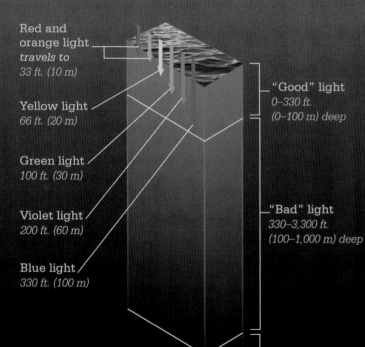

Red and orange light *travels to 33 ft. (10 m)*

Yellow light *66 ft. (20 m)*

Green light *100 ft. (30 m)*

Violet light *200 ft. (60 m)*

Blue light *330 ft. (100 m)*

"Good" light *0–330 ft. (0–100 m) deep*

"Bad" light *330–3,300 ft. (100–1,000 m) deep*

No light *below 3,300 ft. (1,000 m)*

Under pressure

Water pressure increases quickly with depth. At only 33 feet (10 m) down, there is twice the pressure we feel at the surface. In the deepest ocean, it squashes an area the size of a fingernail with the weight of one elephant! Down there, our air-filled lungs would be crushed as small as tennis balls. But the watery fluids inside deep-sea creatures can withstand this huge pressure.

Mojarra grunts
As water pressure grows, these fish stay afloat by increasing the amount of gas in their swim bladders.

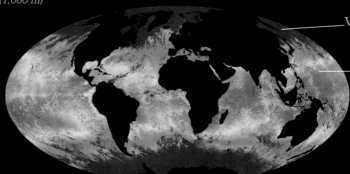

Very cold water

Warmer water

Warm and cold
On this satellite image taken from space, warm water looks red and yellow. Cold water looks blue and green.

Sea temperatures

Tropical waters heat up with the full-on glare of the Sun overhead. Polar waters receive only weak, slanting rays, yet some types of fish, shellfish, and crab are perfectly adapted to the almost-frozen water there.

From light to dark

The sunlit zone at the top of the ocean is home to the most living things. Here, plants use sunlight to live and grow, providing food for many creatures. Deeper down, food is scarce, and animals have to survive on what drifts down from above.

More than **90%** of all water in the oceans is dark and below 43°F (6°C)

Sunlit zone
0–330 ft. (0–100 m)

Teeming with life
Plants such as seaweed and tiny diatoms thrive in the brightness. They are eaten by many different kinds of creatures. Some larger animals come up from the deep to feed here.

DIATOMS

MACKEREL

GREEN TURTLE

Twilight zone
330–3,300 ft. (100–1,000 m)

Getting very dim
As the light fades, animal eyes get bigger to see in the gloom. Only a few deep-diving air breathers, such as elephant seals and sperm whales, can cope with the increasing pressure.

HUMBOLDT SQUID

SPERM WHALES

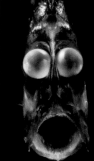
HATCHETFISH

Dark zone
3,300–13,200 ft. (1,000–4,000 m)

Eyes are useless
Long sensory hairs and feelers pick up faint ripples from movements nearby. Having a huge mouth makes it easy to grab victims.

GULPER EEL

SNIPE EEL   HAIRY ANGLERFISH

Abyss and trench
13,200–36,300 ft. (4,000–11,000 m)

Bottom of the world
Life is scarce and slow in the high-pressure, near-freezing blackness. Most animals eat sinking debris, called "marine snow."

HADAL SNAILFISH

GIANT TUBE WORM   TRIPOD FISH

Ancient ocean [Just one]

About 250 million years ago, there was just one ocean, a superocean called Panthalassa. All the land was clustered together, too, in what is now known as the supercontinent Pangaea. The ocean landscape was often changed by exploding volcanoes and earth movements. Strange creatures, both huge and tiny, inhabited the ocean and the skies above.

Maps on the move

Over hundreds of millions of years, Pangaea gradually split up and the continents drifted apart. But the further back we go in time, the less sure we can be of the true outlines of both the land and the sea.

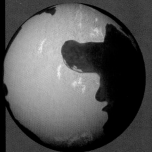

750 million years ago
Supercontinent Rodinia existed at the time of "Snowball Earth," when almost all seas and oceans were iced over.

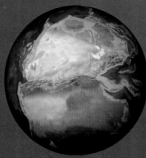

250 million years ago
All continents were jammed together into Pangaea, one-third of the planet's surface. The rest was water—Panthalassa.

160 million years ago
Pangaea started to split into northern Laurasia and Gondwana in the south, with the widening Tethys Sea between.

65 million years ago
The Atlantic had grown, and the other four oceans, and the continents as we know them today, had started to form.

In the future
The Atlantic widens by 1.5–3 in. (4–8 cm) yearly. The Pacific shrinks slightly but is still a third of the Earth's surface.

ORNITHOCHEIRUS

LIOPLEURODON

ICHTHYOSAUR,
STENOPTERYGIUS

CYCLOMEDUSA
JELLYFISH

Sea monster
Liopleurodon, *33 feet (10 m) long,
ruled the seas 150 million years ago. It
is seen here terrorizing another extinct
reptile, an ichthyosaur. The flying reptile*
Ornithocheirus *hovers menacingly above,
while* **Cyclomedusa** *jellyfish move
gracefully through the water.*

Oceans today [Watery world]

The world's salt water is divided into five great oceans. Around most of these are smaller areas of water partly surrounded by land, known as seas. But water flows freely among them, which means that oceans and seas form one vast, continuous body of water—the marine habitat.

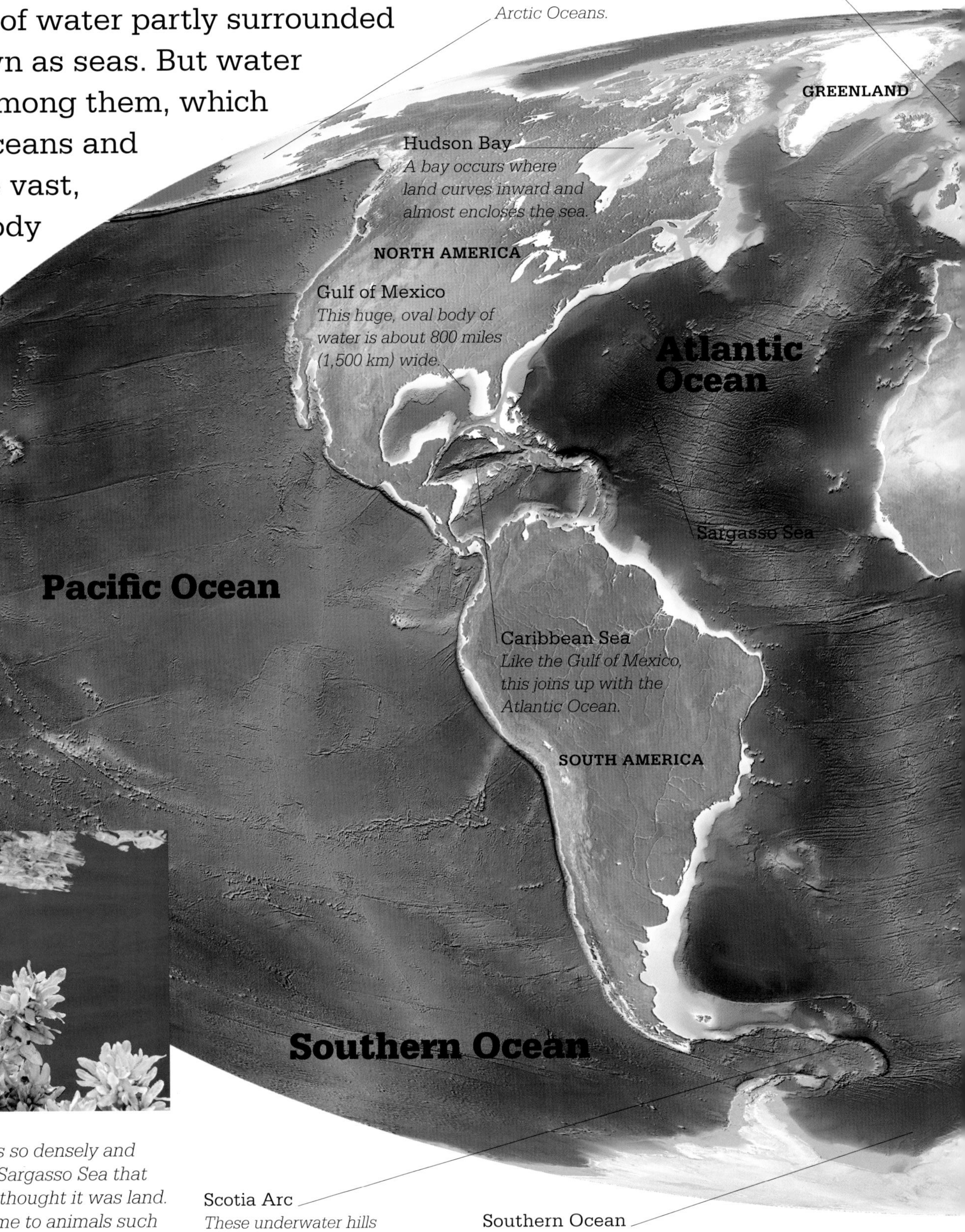

Bering Sea
This icy sea links the Pacific and Arctic Oceans.

North Sea
This is one of the shallowest of the larger seas.

GREENLAND

Hudson Bay
A bay occurs where land curves inward and almost encloses the sea.

NORTH AMERICA

Gulf of Mexico
This huge, oval body of water is about 800 miles (1,500 km) wide.

Atlantic Ocean

Pacific Ocean

Sargasso Sea

Caribbean Sea
Like the Gulf of Mexico, this joins up with the Atlantic Ocean.

SOUTH AMERICA

Southern Ocean

Sargasso Sea
Sargassum weed grows so densely and widely throughout the Sargasso Sea that Christopher Columbus thought it was land. Sargassum weed is home to animals such as shrimps and crabs. Above, a loggerhead turtle takes a rest on it.

Scotia Arc
These underwater hills curve around between South America and Antarctica.

Southern Ocean
The Southern Ocean is formed where the southern parts of the Atlantic, Pacific, and Indian Oceans come together.

Arctic Ocean

Black Sea
The Bosphorus Strait, less than 2.1 miles (3.4 km) wide, joins this to the "Med."

Sea of Okhotsk
The Kamchatka Peninsula and the Kuril Islands separate this from the Pacific.

Saltiest seas
The Dead Sea, between Jordan and Israel, is so salty that almost nothing can live there. The extra salt makes the water so heavy, people can float in it even while reading a book!

Aral Sea
This sea is shrinking fast— a lot of its water has been diverted to grow crops.

EUROPE

Caspian Sea
This sea is more like a lake—it's completely enclosed by land.

Sea of Japan

East China Sea

Dead Sea
This is the lowest-elevation sea, and one of the saltiest.

ASIA

South China Sea
Several nations claim to own this, the biggest of all seas.

Mediterranean Sea
...e of the most isolated ...s, the "Med" joins the ...ntic through the ...ow 9-mile (15 km) ...it of Gibraltar.

Andaman Sea

AFRICA

Arabian Sea
This sea flows into the northern part of the Indian Ocean.

Mariana Trench
This trench is the deepest point of any sea or ocean.

Indian Ocean

AUSTRALIA

Tasman Sea
Australia and New Zealand are separated by this sea, named after explorer Abel Tasman.

Southern Ocean

ANTARCTICA

Antarctica
Antarctica is surrounded by the Southern (or Antarctic) Ocean.

Top Ten Largest Seas

NAME	AREA in sq. miles (sq. km.)
South China Sea	1,360,000 (3,500,000)
Caribbean Sea	1,060,000 (2,750,000)
Mediterranean Sea	965,000 (2,500,000)
Bering Sea	873,000 (2,240,000)
Gulf of Mexico	615,000 (1,600,000)
Sea of Okhotsk	611,000 (1,580,000)
Sea of Japan	377,000 (978,000)
East China Sea	257,000 (660,000)
Andaman Sea	218,000 (559,000)
Black Sea	163,000 (422,000)

What's inside an ocean?

What would an ocean look like if you took out all the water? This picture shows the northern Atlantic Ocean. The ocean floor is like any other land, with slopes, plains, mountains, and valleys. It is constantly reshaped by volcanoes and earthquakes.

THIS AREA IS SHOWN IN THE BIG PICTURE.

Gulf of Maine
In this huge, long bay, deep seabed valleys plunge down more than 1,640 feet (500 m).

Gulf of Saint Lawrence
The Saint Lawrence River from the Great Lakes widens into a big gulf, forming the world's largest estuary.

Cloudy bottom
Fierce deep-ocean currents near Greenland stir up huge amounts of muddy ooze.

Greenland
Mostly covered by ice, Greenland is a huge island in the Atlantic's far north.

Squishy sediment
The ocean floor is covered with a thick layer of ooze, called sediment.

Caribbean Sea
The Caribbean is a large sea, with many islands, at the western edge of the Atlantic.

Deep places
The Puerto Rican Trench is 28,232 feet (8,605 m) deep.

Ocean floor
In recent years, submersibles such as Alvin, left, have enabled us to study the ocean floor at ever-increasing depths. They have revealed "smokers" (hydrothermal vents) and helped scientists discover new creatures.

Bermudan reefs
Bermuda is one large island, Main Island, and 180 small ones, more than 620 miles (1,000 km) from the North American mainland. Coral reefs grow in the warm, shallow waters around Bermuda's coasts.

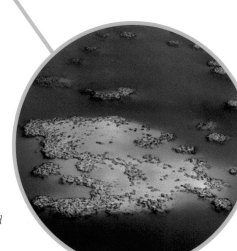

[Terrain]

At **6,200 miles** (10,000 km) long, the Mid-Atlantic Ridge is the largest single physical feature on Earth

Mid-Atlantic Ridge
The Atlantic is getting wider due to new seafloor made at this long row of low mountains.

Iceland
The island of Iceland is at the northern end of the Mid-Atlantic Ridge, which almost splits it in two.

Rockall Plateau
This wide, flat area near Ireland is 4,921 feet (1,500 m) deep. Fish feed and breed here.

North Sea
The British Isles separate the Atlantic Ocean from this cold, shallow sea.

Cape Verde Rise
Sediments around these old underwater volcanoes are over 1 mile (1.6 km) deep.

On the shelf
The area of ocean around most main landmasses is called the continental shelf. Its water is usually less than 490 feet (150 m) deep. There is lots of sunlight, and all kinds of marine life thrive there.

Volcanic beach
The Canary Islands, part of Spain, are 60–300 miles (100–500 km) west of Africa. They are the tips of volcanoes that erupted on the ocean floor. Waves wear down their jagged rocks, creating beaches of dark sand.

Water on the move

The ocean is never still. Even when there are no ripples on top, tides and currents surge beneath. These currents mix water from different oceans, so the same drop of water may, in time, travel around the world.

Currents

When you see things swept along in the water, they are in a current—a mass of water flowing in one direction. Wind and the Earth's turning cause surface currents, but varying temperatures and salt content cause them to change strength and direction below the surface.

← COOL CURRENTS
WARM CURRENTS

A world of currents
The Sun's heat, tides, and winds cause enormous flowing currents around and between the oceans and seas, changing with the seasons. Creatures such as whales, turtles, and sharks "ride" the currents.

Whirlpools
Small-scale but very strong currents form in narrow channels and near obstacles such as piers and islands. This spinning swirl of water, called a whirlpool, is next to the base of a bridge tower.

Water cycle

On land, freshwater is vital for all living things. The Earth does not run out of it because water is always on the move to and from oceans and seas, in a vast, complicated cycle driven by the Sun's warmth. As it evaporates from oceans, the water leaves its salt behind. Then it condenses as clouds and falls as fresh (nonsalty) rain on land.

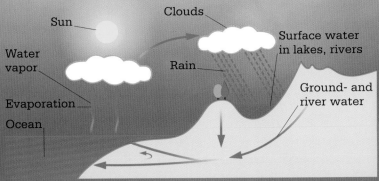

Sun · Clouds · Surface water in lakes, rivers · Water vapor · Rain · Ground- and river water · Evaporation · Ocean

Around and around
Sun-warmed seawater evaporates, or turns to vapor. As it rises, it cools and condenses back into liquid water—as billions of tiny drops that form clouds. These drops fall as rain, or frozen as hail and snow. On land, rainwater flows as streams and rivers, and also seeps down into soil and rocks as groundwater. All of this water eventually flows back into the sea.

Making waves

Waves form when winds blow across the ocean's surface. They are also made when tides and currents push into objects, such as reefs, coasts, and undersea mountains. Waves that do not break are known as swell.

Make, then break
As a wave reaches shallower water, it gets taller and goes faster. Finally, its top curls over, or breaks, in a cloud of spray.

Fun with waves
Surfers, windsurfers, and kitesurfers use waves to gain speed and height for acrobatic tricks—as do dolphins.

Crest (highest point)

Trough (lowest point)

Wave height is measured from crest to trough

Wavelength is measured from crest to crest

Top of wave moves faster

Wave breaks

Returning water from previous wave

Water in a wave moves in circles, not forward or sideways, in open water

Circular motion gets smaller in deep water

Rising seabed affects circular motion and slows down the wave base

Wave top overtakes wave base as wave crests get closer together

Hurricane
These towering, dark-based clouds signal a hurricane—a huge storm that forms over warm ocean water. There are about ten hurricanes each year in the North Atlantic. Most head west and their winds, traveling at more than 75 miles per hour (119 kph), do massive damage around the Caribbean Sea and Gulf of Mexico.

Ocean's edge [Shores galore]

No two shores are the same—from tall, sheer cliffs, to jumbled boulders, to flat, sandy beaches. Each coast depends on the land's rock type and on the ocean's winds, waves, currents, and tides. One big storm can demolish cliffs, pile up boulders, wash away sand, and change the whole coastline overnight.

Up and down the beach

Wind and water reshape sandy beaches every day. But there is usually a berm (ridge) at the high-tide mark, a face (slope) below, and a flatter terrace under the surf or breaking waves. A drop beyond is the low-tide mark.

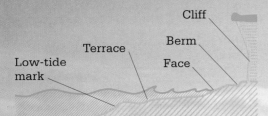

Low-tide mark
Terrace
Cliff
Berm
Face

Side view
The angle of the face depends partly on wave power and currents sweeping past.

What is a tide?

Twice a day, the sea level rises and falls along the coast. These movements are tides. High tide occurs when the water stops rising; low tide happens when it falls back.

Levels
This same place looks completely different during low and high tides.

Making tides

Tides are caused by the gravity (pull) of the Moon, which lifts water into a bulge on the part of the Earth's surface facing it.

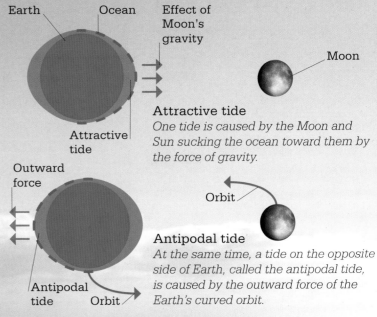

Earth
Ocean
Effect of Moon's gravity
Moon
Attractive tide

Attractive tide
One tide is caused by the Moon and Sun sucking the ocean toward them by the force of gravity.

Outward force
Orbit
Antipodal tide
Orbit

Antipodal tide
At the same time, a tide on the opposite side of Earth, called the antipodal tide, is caused by the outward force of the Earth's curved orbit.

What is sand?

Sand is made up mostly of tiny chunks of the mineral quartz, but it also contains grains of worn-down rocks and shells. Larger chunks are called gravel or pebbles.

Sticky sand

Other minerals give sand different colors. Water helps small grains stick together—ideal for castle building.

SAND GRAINS

MONUMENTAL SAND CASTLE, SAN DIEGO, CA

Amazing beaches

Beaches of the world vary—from tropical sandy ones scattered with colorful shells to those so stony you can't walk on them barefoot.

So long!
Cox's Bazar Beach in Bangladesh is more than 75 miles (120 km) long.

So dazzling!
Hyams Beach, New South Wales, Australia, holds the record for the whitest sand.

So noisy!
Princess Juliana Airport, on St. Maarten in the Caribbean, has a beach right at the end of the runway.

More here

Bamba Beach
by Pratima Mitchell
The Cay
by Theodore Taylor

Botany Bay, Australia
Seychelles **Waikiki beach, Hawaii** Cancun, Mexico

Organize a beach cleanup to get rid of litter and hazards like broken glass, which harm people and wildlife. You may find washed-up treasures!

Don't walk on dunes—they help prevent wind and water erosion. Don't litter—plastics, fishing line, and other trash can kill wildlife.

neap tides: the highest low tides and lowest high tides, which occur when the Moon, Sun, and Earth are not aligned in a straight line.

spring tides: the highest high tides and lowest low tides, which occur when the Moon and Sun pull together in the same direction. Spring tides are not related to the spring season.

Oce
of the

- Which oceans are home to the largest island?

* Who walked on an ocean?

- How do exploding volcanoes make islands?

ans
world

There are five oceans on Earth: the Pacific, the Atlantic, the Indian, the Arctic, and the Southern (or Antarctic). The Pacific is by far the largest, almost as big as all the other oceans and seas put together. Most are surrounded by land, but the Southern merges into three other oceans.

Five big oceans

Each ocean has large seas, gulfs, and bays around its edge, such as the Caribbean Sea west of the Atlantic. The Atlantic only covers two-thirds as much area as the Pacific, but it receives river water from four times more land area than the Pacific does.

North America

ATLANTIC OCEAN

Atlantic Ocean facts

Area	41,100,000 sq. miles (106,400,000 sq. km.)
Deepest point	27,500 ft. (8,380 m)
Coldest sea temperature in middle latitudes	28°F (–2°C)

Atlantic

The second-largest ocean, the Atlantic has fewer islands than the other oceans, but it does have big seas, such as the Mediterranean, and wild, devastating storms, called hurricanes (or sometimes tropical cyclones).

Busy with trade
Enormous cargo ships cross the Atlantic between the Americas, Europe, and Africa, carrying up to half of the world's raw materials, such as oil and mineral ores, and also manufactured goods.

Indian

Mostly warm and with many sheltered areas, the Indian Ocean is home to many island nations, including the Maldives, Madagascar, and Sri Lanka. About 40 percent of the world's offshore oil is from the Indian Ocean.

Coral islands
Coral animals like the Indian Ocean's warm, calm water. Over thousands of years they have built huge, rocky reefs and islands.

Pacific

The Pacific covers almost a third of the Earth's total surface and has more islands—more than 20,000—than all the other oceans combined. Although its name means "peaceful," the Pacific, like the Atlantic, can sometimes be swept by giant storms.

El Niño
This is a climate pattern that occurs across the tropical Pacific about every five years. It accompanies high atmospheric pressure in the western Pacific and can cause huge waves, such as these off Hawaii.

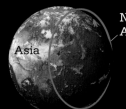

PACIFIC OCEAN

Pacific Ocean facts

Area	63,800,000 sq. miles (165,200,000 sq. km.)
Deepest point	35,797 ft. (10,911 m)
Coldest sea temperature in middle latitudes	32°F (0°C)

INDIAN OCEAN

Indian Ocean facts

Area	28,350,000 sq. miles (73,556,000 sq. km.)
Deepest point	23,812 ft. (7,258 m)
Coldest sea temperature in northern latitudes	72°F (22°C)
Coldest sea temperature in southern latitudes	30°F (–1°C)

SOUTHERN OCEAN

Southern Ocean facts

Area	7,848,222 sq. miles (20,327,000 sq. km.)
Deepest point	23,736 ft. (7,235 m)
Coldest sea temperature	28°F (–2°C)

ARCTIC OCEAN

Arctic Ocean facts

Area	5,427,000 sq. miles (14,056,000 sq. km.)
Deepest point	17,880 ft. (5,450 m)
Coldest sea temperature	28.7°F (–1.8°C)

Southern

The Southern Ocean is not all open water. In winter, great sheets of ice spread out from the Antarctic continent and float on the water. Large pieces of ice often break off the sheets and become icebergs.

Chilling out
Penguins live only in the southern half of the world. After eating shrimplike krill in the sea, these Adélie penguins take a rest on broken, jumbled sea ice, with Antarctica's huge cliffs behind.

Arctic

The Arctic Ocean is the smallest and shallowest of the five oceans. It joins other oceans through only two gaps, one to the Pacific between Russia and Alaska, and one to the Atlantic between Greenland and northern Europe. It is otherwise surrounded by land.

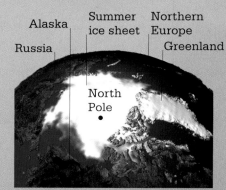

Mostly ice
For much of the winter, the Arctic Ocean is almost entirely covered by a floating sheet of ice about 10–13 feet (3–4 m) thick. In the summer, the ice melts around the edges and shrinks away from the land, as shown above.

The Pacific Ring of Fire
This runs along the landmasses surrounding the Pacific Ocean in a 25,000-mile (40,000 km) horseshoe, where earthquakes shake the ocean floor and volcanic eruptions spurt out red-hot lava, as on the coast of Hawaii (left). The Ring of Fire has 452 (almost 75 percent) of the world's active and dormant volcanoes.

Islands in the sea

Islands are land areas smaller than continents, with water all around them. In the far north and south, ocean islands are windy and icy. Pacific and Indian Ocean islands and some Atlantic ones are warm and sunny. They are often home to animals found nowhere else.

Island types

Some islands are high hills around the edges of continents, where water has flooded the low area between the hill and the mainland. Other islands are the tips of coral reefs, undersea mountains, and volcanoes that erupt on the ocean floor.

"70 Islands," Palau, West Pacific
This tiny group of coral islands has been protected by law for more than 50 years.

An island is born

Most new islands form due to volcanoes or earthquakes. In 1963, a volcano south of Iceland in the North Atlantic Ocean erupted to form the small island of Surtsey.

Early eruption
The volcano was in water 426 feet (130 m) deep, but soon grew to the surface.

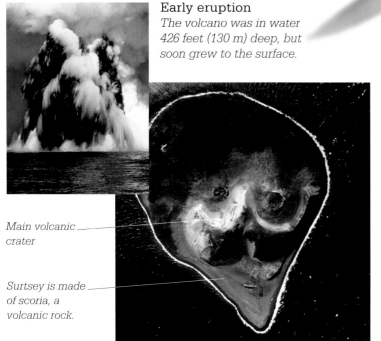

Main volcanic crater

Surtsey is made of scoria, a volcanic rock.

Nowhere else
Some islands have unique animals and plants. Lemurs, like this ring-tailed one, are found only on Madagascar.

All quiet now
Surtsey no longer erupts and is 0.54 square mile (1.4 sq. km.) in size. It now has some plant and animal life. It is gradually being eroded by wind and waves and may disappear by 2150.

Extraordinary islands

There are more than 100,000 islands in the seas and oceans. Each has its own features, weather, and wildlife. The most remote island is Bouvet Island in the South Atlantic. The closest inhabited landmass is South Africa, more than 1,600 miles (2,580 km) away.

Biggest and smallest
At 836,000 square miles (2,166 million sq. km.), mighty Greenland, three times the size of Texas, lies in the Arctic and Atlantic Oceans. Bishop Rock, in the UK's southwest, is the smallest island with a building.

LARGEST ISLAND: GREENLAND   **SMALLEST: BISHOP ROCK**

North and south
In 1900, US explorer Robert Peary discovered Kaffeclubben Island near Greenland, which is the island closest to the North Pole. Down south, Berkner is a completely ice-covered island next to Antarctica.

Berkner island

ROBERT PEARY   **BERKNER ISLAND, ANTARCTICA**

Old and young
Madagascar drifted away from the African mainland almost 90 million years ago. The Fukoto-Kuokanaba undersea volcano near Japan forms temporary islands every few years, most recently in 1986.

BAOBAB TREES, MADAGASCAR   **FUKOTO-KUOKANABA**

HONG KONG

Amazing island facts

1. One in every ten people lives on an island. There is even a word for a strong attraction to islands—*islomania*!

2. The name *Hong Kong* means "fragrant harbor" in Cantonese. This may refer to the incense stored around the harbor in the past, ready for export.

3. The Big Island of Hawaii is the largest island in the United States.

4. Greenland was discovered by Vikings in the 10th century. It is believed that they called it Greenland to entice settlers to live there.

5. Santa Cruz del Islote off the Colombian coast is the most crowded island in the world—1,247 people live in just under 0.0038 square mile (0.1 sq. km.).

6. Manhattan Island's Chinatown is the largest Chinese community outside China.

More here

Treasure Island
by Robert Louis Stevenson
Robinson Crusoe
by Daniel Defoe

volcano Iwo Jima **atoll** Galápagos Islands **barrier island** Rapa Nui **island chains**

Visit your closest island, which could be in a lake or river. See live volcanoes in Hilo, Hawaii. Learn how immigrants entered the United States at New York's Ellis Island. Visit sea caves at Santa Cruz Island in California.

archipelago: a group of islands close together.

atoll: a kind of coral reef island that surrounds a lagoon.

causeway: a bridgelike path, roadway, or railway across water, often between the mainland and a nearby island.

desert island: an island with no inhabitants.

motus: a Polynesian term for tiny islets and bits of broken reef around a main coral island.

Crossing the oceans

The first long-distance sea voyagers probably drifted along on log rafts, perhaps 50,000 years ago. Sailing began in the Mediterranean around 5,000 years ago. By the 1400s, brave explorers set out to sail west across the vast oceans to find new lands, bring home treasures such as gold, and set up trading routes for spices like pepper, which couldn't easily be bought in Europe.

ROUTE KEY
- MAGELLAN
- ERIKSSON
- ZHENG HE
- COOK
- COLUMBUS

GREENLAND

BAFFIN ISLAND (CA.1002)

Leif Eriksson
500 years before Columbus, Icelander Eriksson reached North America.

ICELAND

GODHAVN (CA.1001)

NEWFOUNDLAND (CA.1003)

NORTH AMERICA

PLYMOUTH (1768)

EURO

PALOS DE LA FRONTERA (1

SEVILLA (1519)

Early explorers
People have always fished for food from the sea, but as boats, oars, and sails improved, they ventured farther from shore. Many island cultures have long seafaring traditions, especially across the Pacific Ocean.

Polynesians
People from New Guinea "island-hopped" in small boats to colonize the South Pacific.

Christopher Columbus
This Italian explorer wanted to reach India and the East by sailing west. In October 1492, he sighted a "New World."

CUBA (1492)

CAPE VERDE (1519)

"Following the light of the Sun, we left the old world."
—Christopher Columbus

PTOLEMY'S MAP OF THE WORLD, CA. 150 CE

Flat Earth
For centuries, people trembled at tales of sailing off the edge of a flat world, into the mouth of a giant dragon. But when Portuguese-born Ferdinand Magellan's expedition circled the Earth (1519–22), it provided proof that Earth was a sphere.

SOUTH AMERICA

Atlantic Ocean

CAPE HORN (1520)

Ferdinand Magellan
The Victoria was the only ship from Magellan's expedition to return to Spain—without the explorer, who had died in the Philippines.

Exploring the Arctic

The Arctic is mostly a frozen ocean. In 1893–96, Norwegian Fridtjof Nansen tried to reach the North Pole by drifting through the ice in his ship, the Fram. The boat never made it, but Nansen did explore all over the frozen ocean on foot and on skis.

The East India Companies

Several European nations set up trading companies to bring shiploads of silks, spices, gems, and precious metals from India, Southeast Asia (the East Indies), and China.

The Dutch East India Company		*The East India Company (Britain)*	
Operated	1602–1798	Operated	1600–1874
Chief port	Batavia (Jakarta)	Chief port	Madras (Chennai)
Main trade	Spices	Main trade	Spices, textiles, teas
Fleet size	Up to 4,000	Fleet size	More than 2,000

Some of these companies became so large and powerful, they were like countries: able to invade and take over lands, make laws, and imprison or kill offenders. They also operated their own pirate fleets.

EAST INDIA GALLEON

RUSSIA

ASIA

CHINA

LUIJIAGANG
(1430)

Zheng He

Admiral Zheng led seven huge expeditions from China between 1405 and 1433.

HORMUZ
(1431)

INDIA

PANDUA
(1427)

Compass

This has a moving magnetic needle to help early sailors steer more precisely.

RICA

CEYLON
(1431)

Indian Ocean

JAKARTA AND
SUMATRA (1770)

MALINDI
(1414)

Pacific Ocean

AUSTRALIA

CAPE OF
GOOD HOPE
(1771)

BOTANY BAY
(1770)

YOUNG NICK'S HEAD,
NEW ZEALAND (1769)

Antarctica

In 1820, Fabian von Bellingshausen was the first to see this freezing continent. In 1932, Stanley Kemp was the first to sail around it through icy waters.

James Cook

Captain Cook, from Yorkshire, England, took three long voyages between 1768 and 1779. He mapped vast areas of the South Pacific, including the east coast of Australia, in his ship Endeavour (replica, left).

Southern Ocean

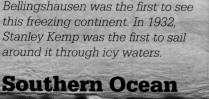

Life in
Oce

- What kind of forest grows 17 inches (45 cm) in a day?

* Which creatures keep the sandy floors clean?

- What is the biggest animal in the ocean?

n the
ean

Kinds of life [What's there?]

Seas and oceans swarm with life of all kinds, from plants too small to see to the world's biggest animal—the blue whale. Some living things are familiar, such as seaweed and dolphins. Others are strange, ranging from slimy, jellylike creatures to hard-cased shellfish. There are still many more living things to discover beneath the waves.

Animals in danger

Many sea creatures are under threat from various causes, including water pollution, overfishing, and harmful waste disposal. Hundreds of types of invertebrates and fish are at risk, including crabs, seahorses, and great white sharks. Mammals in danger include porpoises, dolphins, and whales.

Ocean life

Many creatures on Earth are dependent on the oceans for existence. Marine life is divided mainly into these groups: plants, microscopic life, and animals. The animal group is divided into invertebrates, fish, reptiles, birds, and mammals. Plants use energy from the Sun to live and grow, while animals eat plants, other animals, or both. The most common land creatures, insects, are rarely found in or on the open ocean; only a relative few tolerate saltwater.

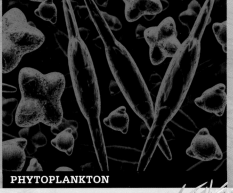
PHYTOPLANKTON

Microscopic

Many ocean plants are smaller than the dot on this i. They are known as phytoplankton and are eaten by tiny creatures called zooplankton. Plankton cover a wide range of sizes.

Plants

The largest plants are seaweed, also known as algae. Some of the biggest are giant kelps. They grow more than 250 feet (80 m) long and can grow 17 inches (45 cm) in a day. They form thick "forests," which are home to many different animals.

KELP FOREST

Invertebrates

These are animals without an inner skeleton or backbone. Most are soft and squishy, like jellyfish, sea anemones, worms, squid, octopuses, and sea slugs. But shellfish, such as crabs and lobsters, have a hard body casing.

SEA ANEMONE

Fish

Most fish have fins and a tail for swimming. They breathe underwater using gills, which absorb oxygen and give off carbon dioxide. Some, such as sharks, are dull colored, while others have brighter colors.

ANGELFISH

Reptiles

The main reptiles in the ocean are sea turtles and sea snakes. They come to the surface often to breathe air. The marine iguana is the only sea-dwelling lizard. The saltwater crocodile is another sea dweller.

GREEN TURTLE

Mammals

Mammals are warm-blooded and breathe air. Full-time sea dwellers include more than 80 kinds of whale, dolphin, and porpoise, as well as manatees and dugongs. Seals and sea lions feed in the sea but breed on land.

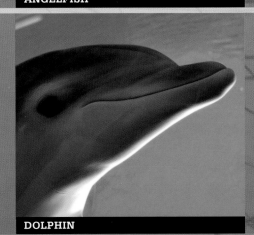
DOLPHIN

Seabirds

Hundreds of birds, from huge albatross to colorful puffins, fly over the sea and feed there. They catch fish, squid, and other near-surface animals. Penguins cannot fly at all, but, like puffins, they use their wings to speed through the water after prey.

PUFFIN

Food webs [What eats what!]

Chain of energy

Most life on Earth gets its energy from the Sun. Ocean plants use sunlight to make food. These plants are eaten by animals, which in turn are eaten by other animals, transferring the energy.

The Sun
The Sun shining on the ocean provides the energy for the food chain.

Phytoplankton
Tiny drifting plants such as diatoms capture the Sun's light energy and use it to live, grow, and breed.

Krill
These shrimplike animals filter the water to catch and eat phytoplankton. In this way, they take in and use energy that was once sunlight.

Great whales
As krill filter-feed on plankton, great whales filter-feed on krill. The sunlight's energy has now reached the third link in the food chain.

Most sea creatures have a favorite food; they then become the favorite food of bigger, stronger animals. Energy is transferred when one animal eats another, forming a food chain. Food chains link together to make food webs, in which many different creatures eat many different things in an ecosystem.

Antarctic food web

Here are a few of the feeding links in Antarctic waters. Follow the arrows to find out what animals feed on phytoplankton, then what eats those animals, and so on, until you get to the most powerful predator. The arrows show the transfer of energy and nutrients around the web.

Zooplankton herbivores
Some zooplankton (tiny floating animals) eat phytoplankton.

Squid
These active predators chase a variety of prey, from zooplankton to fish.

Sperm whales
The world's largest predators like to eat squid of all kinds, even giant and colossal ones, and also octopuses and skates.

Penguins
Some penguins eat fish; others prefer krill.

Elephant seals
These enormous hunters eat squid and fish (and even an occasional penguin).

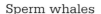

ENERGY FROM
THE SUN

Phytoplankton
This is the base of most ocean food webs.

Web in danger
If one part of the food web is endangered, so is the rest. The krill population has declined by 80 percent in the last few years, so the populations of the animals that eat them may decline also.

Zooplankton carnivores
Some zooplankton feed on their plant-eating cousins.

Krill feeding
Global warming has led to the decline of the krill population.

Krill
Most krill eat phytoplankton but can also eat tiny zooplankton.

Seals
Most seals grab what they can, from large zooplankton and fish to birds.

Seabirds
Different seabirds eat fish, krill, and even zooplankton.

Fish
Like squid, fish are the middle link in many different food chains.

Leopard seals
Fast, strong leopard seals eat penguins and other seals.

Humpback whales
Krill is the main food for these huge whales. They also eat phytoplankton and a variety of smaller fish.

Killer whales
These eat a varied diet, from fish and seals to seabirds and whale calves.

Sand life [On and in]

As the tide goes out at the beach, the damp sand may seem bare and boring. But look closer. Holes, squiggles, and burrows show that worms, shellfish, and other creatures live underneath, hidden among the sandy grains.

Cool home
This hole leads into the crab's safe burrow, which can go down as deep as 4 feet (1.2 m).

On the surface
From tiny flies and hard-cased crabs to tall wading birds, many animals scrape and dig to get at the sand dwellers below. Marram grass stops sand dunes from being blown away.

HERMIT CRAB

HORSESHOE CRABS

MARRAM GRASS

ROBBER FLY

BLACK-BELLIED PLOVER

SANDHILL CRANES

There are
75 million millio

Ghost crabs

Pale-colored and active at night, millions of ghost crabs scurry across warmer sandy shores. They eat anything, from dead fish to rotting seaweed. Then they wave their pincers at one another, pushing and shoving to take over the best beach burrows.

In the sand

From large shellfish to microworms, the sand teems with life. The sea washes up some creatures, and some burrow deep at low tide. The microworms filter feed and scavenge through the sand, cleaning it as they go.

RAZOR CLAMS

MYSTACOCARIDS

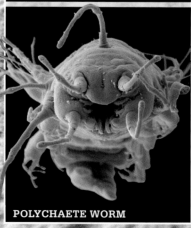

POLYCHAETE WORM

million grains of sand on all the world's beaches

Ready to lay
Flapping its flippers like a bird's wings, a green turtle "flies" over the sandy seabed of the West Pacific Ocean. When night falls, she will haul herself up the beach, dig a hole with her flippers, lay more than 100 eggs, cover them with sand, and head back into the sea. She and her babies will be lucky to survive, as people illegally kill turtles for their shells and meat, harvest turtle eggs, and destroy turtle nesting beaches.

More here

📖

Yertle the Turtle
by Dr. Seuss

Kurma the giant
turtle of Hindu
myths
Urashima Tarō
myth from Japan
The Mock Turtle
in Lewis Carroll's
*Alice's Adventures
in Wonderland*

🖱

WIDECAST
leatherback **loggerhead**
Hattes Beach, French
Guiana **reptile**
migration **terrapin**

✓

Support SeaWorld, which
rescues stranded sea
turtles. Follow sea turtle
journeys being tracked by
satellite at www.seaturtle.
org/tracking. Respect
signs saying "Keep
Away: Turtle Breeding
Beach."

❗

Do not buy vacation
souvenirs, keepsakes, or
gifts that could be made
from turtle parts,
especially shells.

Ⓦ

Chelonia: the scientific
order that includes turtles
and tortoises.

carapace: the domed upper
part of a turtle's shell.

plastron: the lower part of a
turtle's shell—its "belly."

Hard-shore life [Hanging on]

Hard shores, made up of rocks and boulders, are tough places to survive. Huge waves crash, rolling rocks and boulders, and never-ending tides bring surging seawater, then leave animals high and dry in the sun and wind. Seaweed here need to be strong and leathery, and creatures need thick skin and quick reflexes to escape injury.

Seaweed

Many seaweed, sometimes called algae, cling to rocks with rootlike suckers called holdfasts. Even if big waves tear them apart, they can soon grow back.

Bladderwrack
Found in the Atlantic and Pacific Oceans, this was the original source of iodine.

Green hair weed
The bright green of this seaweed is due to the presence of a pigment called chlorophyll.

Thongweed
This edible seaweed may be found on exposed shores and only lives for two or three years at the most.

On the rocks

Animals adapt to hard shores because a rich source of food is next door in the sea. Some birds fly high and dive for fish, squid, and similar creatures, while others peck at washed-up dead bodies.

Rock pools
Just like the wide ocean, the miniworld of the rock pool contains fierce predators and worried prey. Each new high tide refreshes the water and brings more food.

Sea anemones
Sea anemones (above and left) are predatory animals that catch small prey. The little red shrimp climbing the rock above may be in big danger!

Thatched barnacles
Barnacles are usually found attached to rocks on steep shores next to seas with powerful currents.

Starfish
These open and eat shellfish.

Marine iguana

The only ocean-going lizard is the marine iguana, which is found on the Galápagos Islands in the Pacific. It dives from sun-warmed rocks into the cool sea to chomp on seaweed. It can hold its breath underwater for up to 20 minutes. After climbing out, it sunbathes to warm up, then dives into the water again.

Guillemot gang

In late spring, these seabirds crowd together to lay their eggs on steep rocks and cliff ledges. Few predators can reach the nests there. Even if they do, hundreds of guillemots flap, squawk, and attack intruders with their sharp, fearsome beaks.

Lagoons [Quiet waters]

Lagoons are shallow and sheltered bodies of water, separated from the sea by sandbars or reefs. They are peaceful places, with few large predators, and are ideal habitats for many odd creatures, such as sea cucumbers. These animals have no true brains, and relay hormone messages to one another through the water.

Types of lagoons

Reef lagoons are fringed by low mounds of rocky coral, often with ocean all around. Coastal lagoons next to land may be bordered by coral reefs, sandbars, pebbled spits, or rocky outcrops.

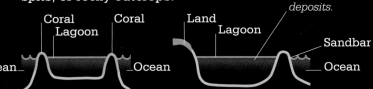

Coral reef lagoon
Coral ridges, which may show above the surface at low tide, protect the lagoon from the open sea.

Coastal saline lagoon
As the Sun evaporates water, the amount of salt in the lagoon may become greater than the amount in the surrounding sea.

Calm water
Protected against big waves, the settled water can become cloudy with fine deposits.

Slimy sausage
Up to 2 feet (60 cm) long, the leopard sea cucumber feeds on rotting matter that floats near the seabed. Clumsy and fleshy, it seems like a juicy target. But its spots warn that its flesh tastes disgusting. And if in danger, it can shoot out its sticky guts to distract an attacker!

Sticky strings
The animal squirts mucus threads to deter predators.

Leopard spots
The bright spots discourage predators from attacking.

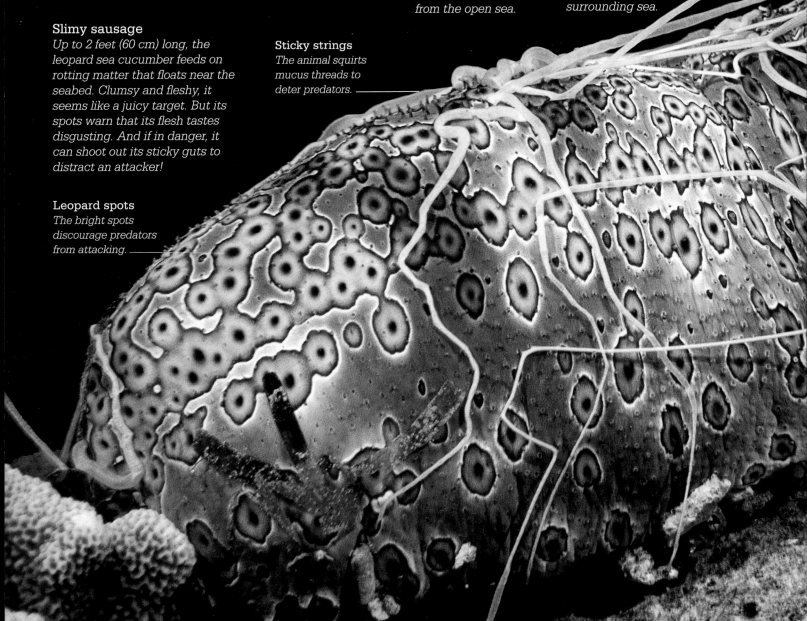

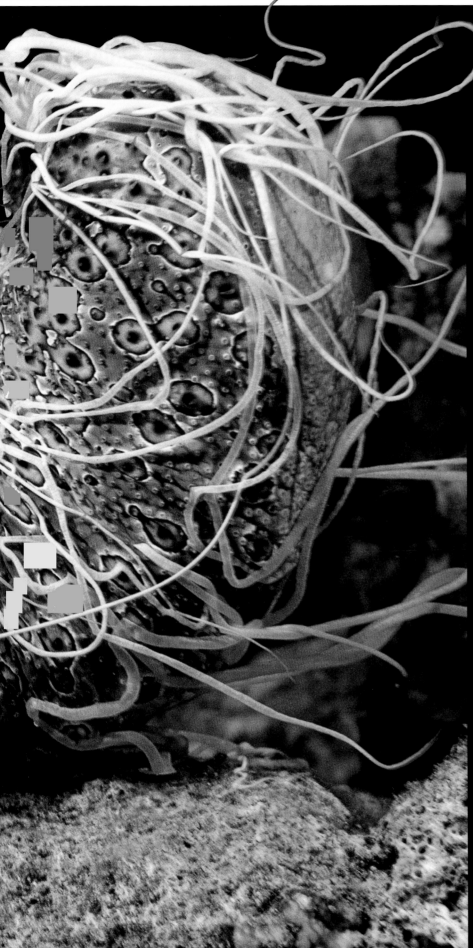

A sheltered life

In the calm lagoon, all sizes of
creatures go about their business.
The 10-foot (3 m) dugong, or sea cow,
can weigh half a ton, and some sea slugs
are smaller than your little finger.

Reef stars
*Starfish are slow
but deadly, preying
on corals or shellfish.
They can turn their
stomachs inside out
to digest their
victims!*

Giant vacuum
*The dugong's main food is sea grass, which it
plows up with its muscular, downturned snout.*

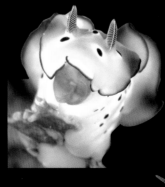

Super slug
*The nudibranch
(meaning "naked
gills") has bright
colors to warn
of its foul taste.*

Wave good-bye
*The anemone's
stinging tentacles
trap fish, shrimps,
and other prey.*

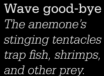

Life in the coral reef

Rain forest of the sea
*Coral reefs support more species than any other ocean habitat.
They are a source of food and medicine for hundreds of millions
of people, and they protect coastlines from erosion. Climate
change, pollution, and overfishing are causing their rapid
decline. About 20 percent of reefs are damaged beyond repair,
and half of those remaining may collapse unless we act soon.*

[Forests of the sea]

Coral reefs, found mainly in tropical seas, are built by colonial animals called corals. Each individual within a colony is a polyp, which grows a tough outer skeleton. When the polyp dies, its skeleton remains. Over time, polyps build up reefs, giving shelter to many animals.

Hidey-holes

A reef's many cracks and crevices make great hiding places and feeding grounds for small fish, shrimps, and similar creatures. Sea slugs and clams cling to the coral.

CAMOUFLAGED SEA HORSE

CLOWN FISH AND SEA ANEMONE

Helpful friends
Many animals help one another on reefs. Cleaner shrimps get leftover food from a moray eel's mouth; the eel gets a cleaning.

1/4 of all marine fish species live in coral reefs

Types of coral

There are two types of corals—stony corals, which make reefs, and soft corals. Stony corals have a single row of tentacles. Soft corals contain spiny skeletal parts called sclerites.

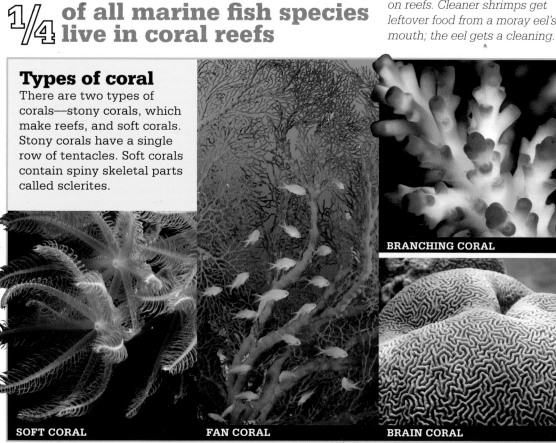

BRANCHING CORAL

SOFT CORAL

FAN CORAL

BRAIN CORAL

More here

The Coral Island
by R. M. Ballantyne
Journey Under the Sea
by Linda Pitkin

Andros Barrier Reef
brain coral **Great Barrier Reef** clams **Belize Barrier Reef** moray eel

Never touch a reef, as you will damage its delicate animals. Stay off the bottom, as stirred-up sediments will smother the coral. Avoid buying reef souvenirs.

Visit the Monterey Bay Aquarium in Monterey, California; or the John G. Shedd Aquarium in Chicago, Illinois; or the Audubon Aquarium of the Americas in New Orleans, Louisiana.

polyp: an individual coral animal that looks like a miniature sea anemone.

symbiosis: an interaction between two organisms living close together, usually beneficial to both. The relationship between a sea anemone and a clown fish is helpful to both animals (the anemone protects the fish from predators, and the fish keeps the anemone's tentacles clean), but parasitism, also a form of symbiosis, is not.

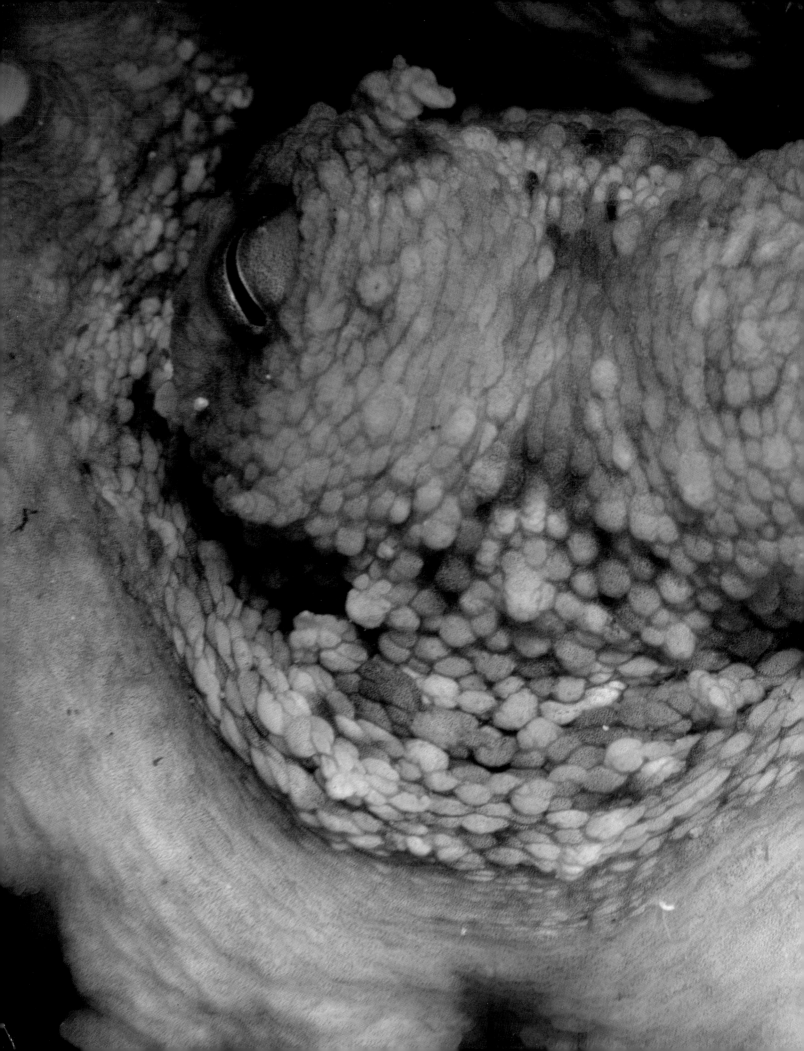

Octopus

This powerful, eight-armed creature peers out from its rocky nest on the seabed. The tentacles (arms) of a common octopus can be more than 3 feet (1 m) long. The octopus is very intelligent, and paralyzes its prey with nerve poison.

Frozen poles [In the freezer]

The icy oceans at the top and bottom of the Earth have some of the weirdest wildlife. Sea temperatures fall below freezing during months of winter darkness, followed by endless daylight in summer. Fearsome storms are possible at any time. Yet the waters are rich in nutrients, so creatures have adapted to the harsh conditions.

Arctic and Antarctic
Polar bears can never hunt penguins—they live at opposite ends of the world. Both poles have many kinds of whales, seals, and birds.

Polar bear
With perfect camouflage for snow and ice, this bear catches mainly seals.

Penguin
Unable to fly, these amazing swimmers feed on fish, squid, and krill.

Polar life
The polar regions are home to many kinds of life. The water teems with fish, marine mammals, and more, while birds swim in the freezing waters or fly above.

Invertebrates
Polar animals with no backbones include starfish, jellyfish, and sea anemones. In the brief summer, plankton thrive in the water. They are food for krill, which in turn feed many larger animals.

KRILL   GOLDEN STARFISH   ARCTIC JELLYFISH

Fish
Fish living nearer the surface of the water tend to be more active than those living near the bottom. Bottom dwellers tend to be sluggish, to save their energy.

GREENLAND SHARK   ICEFISH

Birds
These are the creatures that travel closest to the North and South Poles. Many scavenge if given the chance, picking at the floating dead bodies of fish, whales, and seals.

PINTADO PETREL   GENTOO PENGUINS   GLAUCOUS GULL

The wingless midge is the largest land animal of Antarctica

✶ ANTARCTIC WINGLESS MIDGE, ACTUAL SIZE

Whiskery walrus
This enormous Arctic seal cousin weighs almost 2 tons. It feels on the dark seabed with its 500-plus whiskers for shellfish, crabs, and shrimps.

Mammals
To keep warm in subzero-degree waters, seals and whales have a thick layer of fat under their skin called blubber. Seals also have thick, furry coats.

HARP SEAL

WALRUS

LEOPARD SEAL

BELUGA WHALE

RIGHT WHALE

KILLER WHALES

POLAR BEAR

Penguin power

At 4 feet (120 cm) tall and more than 77 pounds (35 kg), emperors are by far the biggest penguins. They can waddle more than 70 miles (113 km) over Antarctic ice, from the sea to their traditional breeding areas—and back again.

Seabirds [What's up there?]

Oceans are a vast source of food for thousands of kinds of birds, from tiny terns to huge sea eagles. Some prefer fish; others chase squid or shrimps. Many scavenge on dead creatures floating in the waves or washed up along the seashore.

Southern oceans

All penguins live south of the Equator, some as far south as Antarctica. They cannot fly, but they are great swimmers. Their wings act like flippers in the water.

ROCKHOPPER PENGUIN   **PENGUIN COLONY**

Mostly airborne

The greatest long-distance fliers are albatross, which soar for many months without landing, even on water. Like fulmars and petrels, they come to land only to lay eggs and raise chicks.

GIANT PETREL

FULMAR

SHEARWATER

BLACK-BROWED ALBATROSS

Colorful feet

The blue-footed booby is common on the Galápagos Islands. The males use their bright blue feet to "dance" and impress females during courtship.

Using land

Some seabirds can feed, and even "sleep," in the air. But most rest on land, and nest there, too, along coasts and seashores, and even on tiny, remote islands. Dry ground is also a place to clean beaks, feed, and preen feathers.

FRIGATE BIRDS

GANNET

PELICANS

CORMORANT

SANDPIPER

SKIMMER

TUFTED PUFFIN

BLACK-BACKED GULL

BLACK GUILLEMOTS

BLACK TERN

Fish [Fins, scales, tails . . .]

More than 16,700 different species of fish swim in the oceans, from the huge whale shark at 41.5 feet (12.7 m) long to tiny wrasses and gobies. Most have skeletons inside, breathe using gills, are covered in scales, and move using fins and tails.

Jawless fish

Two kinds of fish, hagfish and lampreys, have no jaws for biting. Instead, their mouths are shaped like a sucker or slit, with small hooks or teeth to scrape flesh.

HAGFISH   **LAMPREY MOUTH**

Strange skeletons

Sharks, skates, rays, and chimaeras (ratfish) form a group called cartilaginous fish. Their skeletons are made not of bone but of a lighter, more flexible substance known as cartilage, or gristle.

SKATE   **ELEPHANT RATFISH**

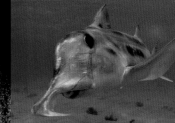

EAGLE RAY   **MANTA RAY**

GREAT WHITE SHARK

Deadly fish
The fierce-looking reef stonefish of Southeast Asia and Australia is the world's most poisonous fish. Its back spines inject a powerful venom that can kill a person in a few hours.

Bony fish

Fish with skeletons made of bone are by far the biggest group. Some are sleek, silvery hunters. Others are brightly colored coral reef dwellers, or they may be flattened and camouflaged to lie unseen on the seabed.

HERRING "BAIT-BALL"

ATLANTIC COD

PORCUPINE FISH

LEAFY SEA DRAGON

FLYING FISH

PEACOCK FLOUNDER

SUNFISH

PACIFIC SAILFISH

BOXFISH

ORANGE-SPOT GOBY

ORNATE WRASSE

MORAY EEL

From species smaller than your hand to some bigger than a bus, more than 430 kinds of shark cruise the seas. All eat meat, from taking bites out of giant whales to crushing hard-cased shellfish. Strangely, the largest sharks eat the smallest food—tiny floating plankton.

Shark sizes

More than two-thirds of sharks are in the 3-to-10-foot (1 to 3 m) range. The vast whale shark sieves surface plankton; the dwarf lanternshark snacks on small fish.

DWARF LANTERNSHARK 7 IN. (17 CM)

Great white
White pointer, man-eater, and white death are a few names for the biggest predatory shark. It prefers to eat seals and dolphins.

GREAT WHITE SHARK 19.6 FT. (6 M)

WHALE SHARK 41.5 FT. (12.7 M)

Tail types

Fast-cruising sharks have almost equal top and bottom tail lobes (the two parts of the tail fin). Sprinting sharks have bigger upper lobes.

1 PORBEAGLE

2 SANDBAR SHARK

3 GANGES SHARK

4 NURSE SHARK

5 TIGER SHARK

6 ZEBRA SHARK

7 THRESHER SHARK

8 BASKING SHARK

9 GREAT WHITE SHARK

10 COOKIE-CUTTER SHARK

Sharks and humans

Shark attacks are big news—partly because they are so rare. Yet it is estimated that 100 million sharks are killed by people every year, due to commercial and recreational fishing. Millions are killed cruelly for their fins, to make shark fin soup. Fins sell illegally for huge sums.

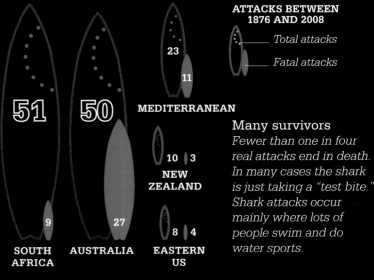

92

51

50

23

11

MEDITERRANEAN

ATTACKS BETWEEN 1876 AND 2008
— Total attacks
— Fatal attacks

8
WESTERN US

9
SOUTH AFRICA

27
AUSTRALIA

10 | 3
NEW ZEALAND

8 | 4
EASTERN US

Many survivors
Fewer than one in four real attacks end in death. In many cases the shark is just taking a "test bite." Shark attacks occur mainly where lots of people swim and do water sports.

In its lifetime, a great white has

20,000

teeth (you'll have about 50)

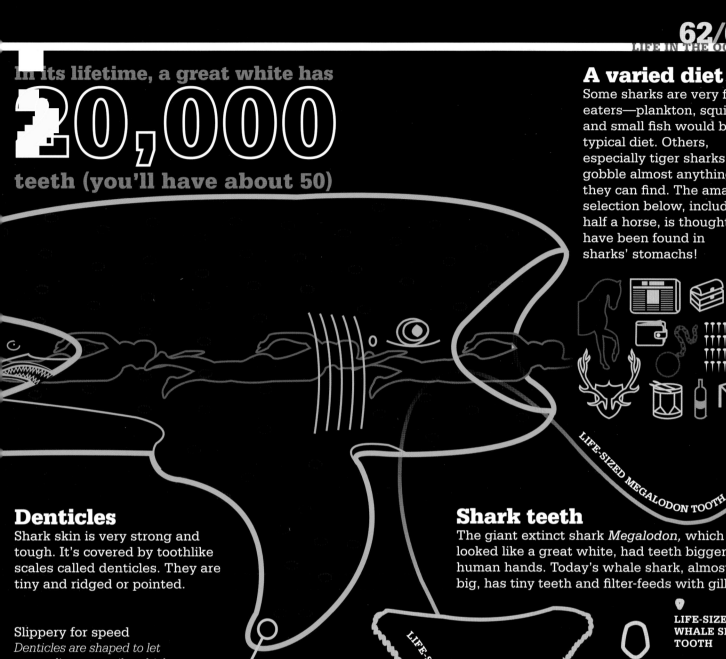

A varied diet

Some sharks are very fussy eaters—plankton, squid, and small fish would be a typical diet. Others, especially tiger sharks, gobble almost anything they can find. The amazing selection below, including half a horse, is thought to have been found in sharks' stomachs!

LIFE-SIZED MEGALODON TOOTH

Denticles

Shark skin is very strong and tough. It's covered by toothlike scales called denticles. They are tiny and ridged or pointed.

Slippery for speed
Denticles are shaped to let water slip past easily, which allows the shark to swim faster, using less energy.

Tiny swirls of water above skin reduce friction

ROWS OF DENTICLES

Water flows smoothly around denticle

"Side wing" on denticle

Denticle stalk

RAISED DESIGN

Shark teeth

The giant extinct shark *Megalodon*, which looked like a great white, had teeth bigger than human hands. Today's whale shark, almost as big, has tiny teeth and filter-feeds with gills.

LIFE-SIZED WHALE SHARK TOOTH

LIFE-SIZED HUMAN TOOTH

LIFE-SIZED GREAT WHITE TOOTH

What's going on?

Sharks are not just fearsome eating machines. Scientists now believe that they are sophisticated creatures. Many have problem-solving skills, show social skills, and even display curiosity in some situations.

New teeth grow at rear of jaw

Lower jaw (mandible)

Replacement teeth move forward

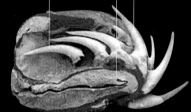

Never-ending supply
Sharks keep growing new teeth. They appear at the back of the jaw and move forward, replacing those that are broken or lost.

Humpback, flipper arms

The humpback whale is named for its dorsal fin, which often has a hump. The hump is noticeable when the whale arches its back to leap out of the water. Whales are mammals, and they can be divided into two groups: those with teeth, and those, like the humpback, with baleen, a filter in the mouth that traps small creatures.

Whale stats [Really big ones!

Baleen whales are the planet's biggest creatures. Of the 12 or more species of baleens, the greatest is the blue whale (*Balaenoptera musculus*), which breaks just about every size record. This giant is the largest animal ever to live on the planet. Its amazing qualities include a tongue that weighs as much as an elephant, and a breathing spout, or "blow," that shoots more than 33 feet (10 m) into the air!

Straining to feed

When feeding, a blue whale lunges at groups of krill, taking them—plus thousands of gallons of water—into its mouth. It then squeezes the water out through its baleen plates and swallows the trapped krill.

Baleen
From the blue whale's upper jaw hangs a "curtain" of around 300 fringed, 3-foot-long (1 m) baleen plates. Acting like a vast sieve, they filter small animals from the water.

Whaling for underwear
Whales have always been hunted for meat and oil, and for 300 years baleen was used to strengthen items such as women's corsets. Commercial whaling was banned in 1986.

Just how big?

You can't put a whale on the scales. At the time when whales were routinely hunted, they were cut up and weighed in pieces. The largest female blue whale measured in this way weighed 195 tons.

An adult blue whale can eat up to

2,000,000
krill a day

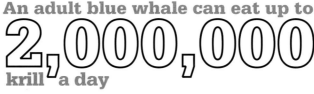

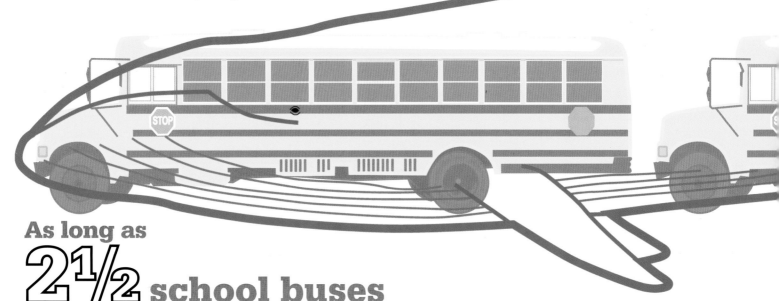

As long as
2½ school buses

A blue whale calf can gain (90 kg) 200 lbs. in weight a day on its mother's rich milk

Side eyed

A great whale's eyes are on the sides of its head, so it has almost no vision ahead or behind. Sight is limited anyway in murky water or at night—hearing is a much more important sense for these creatures.

Megapump

The blue whale's heart is the size of a small car, weighs 1,300 pounds (600 kg), and pumps more than 11 tons of blood. The main artery, the aorta, has a diameter of 9 inches (23 cm)—wider than a soccer ball. The heart beats only five or six times per minute when the whale is at the surface, and even more slowly when it dives down.

LIFE-SIZED CROSS SECTION OF HUMAN AORTA

High capacity

Each time a blue whale's heart beats, it pumps around 635 pints (300 liters) of blood, which is more than two full-to-the-brim bathtubs.

LIFE-SIZED CROSS SECTION OF BLUE WHALE AORTA

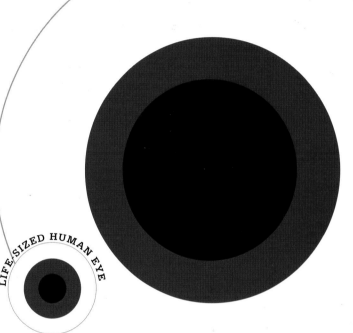

LIFE-SIZED HUMAN EYE

LIFE-SIZED BLUE WHALE EYE

A whale's eye

A blue whale's eyeball is the size of a grapefruit, which is relatively small for such a giant body. The lens is almost spherical and is able to focus in the low light levels near the ocean's surface.

as heavy as 24 bull African elephants

Biggest ever

*In weight, the blue whale easily beats the heaviest dinosaurs, such as **Argentinosaurus**. This plant-eating giant, which lived more than 90 million years ago, is thought to have weighed around 99 tons.*

Deep-sea life [Weird stuff]

Animals that live in the cold, dark, abyssal depths of the sea are some of the strangest on the planet. It's not by accident that they look weird—they have had to develop special features to survive in a very unfriendly habitat. Harsh conditions include inky darkness, very high pressure, freezing temperatures, and the occasional jet of boiling water.

Invertebrates

There are all kinds of invertebrates (animals without backbones) in the deep, from crustaceans to starfish, from worms to octopuses, squid, and jellyfish.

Giant isopod
Scientists are not sure why some animals living at great depths grow bigger than their shallow-water cousins. This woodlouse-type crustacean can grow to 16 inches (40 cm) in length.

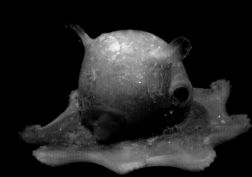

Dumbo octopus
This octopus has giant earlike fins on top of its head, which make it look like the flying elephant in the classic Disney film.

Giant tube worm
The giant tube worm does not depend on sunlight as its source of energy. Instead, it feeds on tiny bacteria that live inside its body.

Fish

Tricks used by deep-sea fish to survive at great depths include making their own light—bioluminescence—to attract prey and mates and to camouflage themselves against predators.

Hairy angler
With a glowing lure dangling above its mouth, this anglerfish attracts prey. Then it sucks its victim in with its extra-large mouth. The hairs on its body can sense objects nearby.

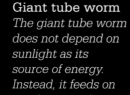

Snipe eel
This eel has about 750 vertebrae (backbones) in its long body—more than any other animal on Earth. It is so slender that it is 75 times as long as it is wide!

Fangtooth
The huge teeth of the fangtooth are no good for chewing or crushing. Instead, they grip on to prey and swallow it whole! Two fangs on the lower jaw are so huge that the fish needs sockets in its upper jaw to contain them.

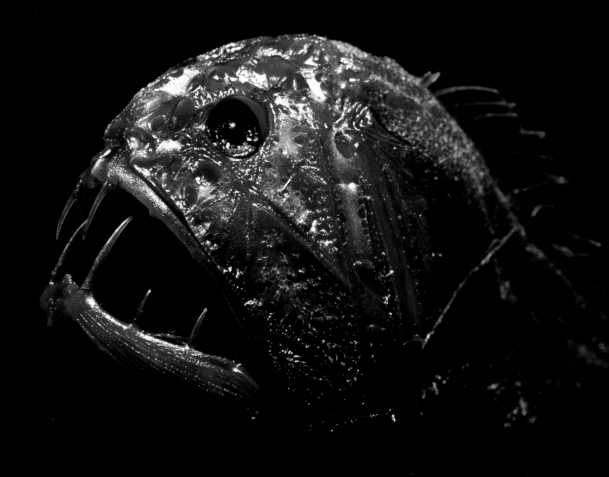

Hagfish
A true monster of the deep, the hagfish attaches itself to a passing fish, bores inside it, and then eats it from the inside out!

Unlike fish living in shallower waters, deep-sea fish don't have swim bladders, as they would collapse under the pressure

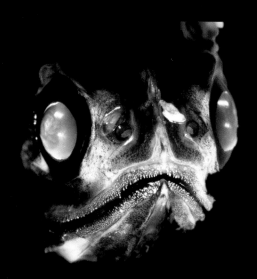

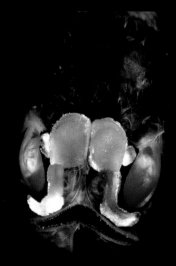

All lit up
Lanternfish (far left and center) and hatchetfish (left) use bioluminescence to attract prey and as a mating signal. They have photophores (light-producing organs) on their bellies, heads and tails.

Peop

oce

-- How does an earthquake cause a giant wave?

* Who set fire to his beard instead of shaving it?

-- What kind of bell is useful underwater?

e and
ans

On the water [World traders]

About 90 percent of all world trade— from freshly cut flowers to giant trucks—travels by sea. Fishing is also a huge ocean industry. Fish are transported in iced containers across the seas, and communities also trade fish with local neighbors.

A living from the sea
The Madagascan Vezo, "people who fish," make their living from fishing. They eat the fish they catch and also sell or trade it for other goods.

Early merchants

Seafaring trade made nations rich and powerful. About 3,000 years ago, the Phoenicians ruled the Mediterranean and Red Seas. 1,000 years ago, Venetians spread their trading empire far and wide, while Chinese cargo ships sailed west to Southeast Asia and India. In the 1600s, Europeans began a rich trade with Asia in silks, spices, and teas.

A good catch
Fleets of fishing boats traded fish in classical times, 2,000 years ago. The Roman fleet reached most parts of its empire.

Major traders

Name	Trading area	Dates	Major goods
Phoenicians	Eastern Mediterranean, Africa, Europe	1400–200 BCE	Wood, precious metals, dyes, textiles
Arab empires	Middle East, South Asia, Africa, Europe	600–1250 CE	Ivory, hardwoods, textiles, spices, slaves
Venetians (Venice)	Mediterranean and Red Seas, Middle East	900–1700	Spices, herbs, silks and other textiles, gems, precious metals, porcelain
Hanseatic League	Northern Europe, eastern Atlantic to Baltic Sea	1250–1650	Textiles, foods, timber, furs, metals, minerals
Somali traders	Eastern and southern Africa, Middle East, South Asia, China	1300s–1600s	Exotic animals, foods, ivory, textiles, spices, gold, weapons, porcelain, furs, metals, minerals

Bulk or container?

Today's ships carry cargoes in two main ways. Bulk goods such as oil, natural gas, grain, and coal are loaded using shovels, pipes, chutes, and tubes. Container ships carry items packed into large metal boxes called containers.

Stack

Standard ship containers are 20 feet (6.1 m) long. They can be stacked like bricks and unloaded quickly, to be taken away by trucks or railroads and unpacked later.

A container ship by the numbers

Name	*Emma Maersk*
Class (type of ship)	E class (8 "sister ships" that are the world's biggest container ships)
Length	1,302 ft. (397 m)
Beam (width)	184 ft. (56 m)
Draft (depth below water)	51 ft. (15.5 m)
Speed	29 mph (47 kph)
Crew	13 (plus 17 passengers)
Load	14,700 standard containers (which could hold almost 100 million cell phones!)
Total weight, fully loaded	187,393 tons
Due 2015	Triple-E class (can take 18,000 containers!)

Singapore to Europe
This busy route through the Panama Canal takes three to four weeks.

Busy seaports

Huge cargo ships sail from the world's seaports every day. The busiest one is Shanghai, handling over 661 million tons of cargo a year!

1. Shanghai
Each year, 30 million standard containers pass through this huge port in China.

2. Singapore
Ships leave Singapore, in Southeast Asia, for 600 other ports worldwide.

3. Rotterdam
This gigantic port in the Netherlands is the largest in Europe—it covers 40 square miles (100 sq. km.).

Shipping routes
Today, most cargo travels between East Asia, North America, and Europe via the Panama Canal, but only ships up to 967 feet (295 m) long and 105 feet (32 m) wide can fit through its locks.

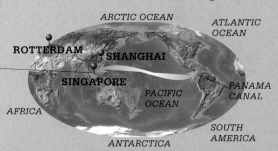

ARCTIC OCEAN
ATLANTIC OCEAN
ROTTERDAM   SHANGHAI
SINGAPORE
PANAMA CANAL
PACIFIC OCEAN
AFRICA
SOUTH AMERICA
ANTARCTICA

Water sports [Splash!]

Instead of just lazing on the beach, you can enjoy sports in or on the sea. You can swim, dive, snorkel, scuba dive, and fish in the sea, or surf, sail, and ski on it. One sport, free diving, involves holding your breath underwater as long as you can—don't try it!

Try it and sea

Many people try sea sports like windsurfing or parasailing when on vacation, but it may not be practical to do them regularly. The best way is to join a group or club that provides training, safety advice, and equipment rental.

Diving deep
The deepest scuba divers can go down more than 1,000 ft. (310 m).

Some popular water sports

	Estimated number of participants worldwide
Sea fishing	At least 50 million
Sailing (inshore)	Up to 50 million
Surfing	Up to 25 million
Scuba diving	20-plus million
Windsurfing (sailboarding)	19–20 million
Kite surfing	Up to 5 million
Wakeboarding (waterskiing with a board)	3–3.5 million
Ocean sailboat racing	Fewer than 1 million
Free diving (breath holding)	About 200,000
Offshore powerboat racing	About 30,000

An America's Cup sailboat costs more than
$10 million

THE AMERICA'S CUP TROPHY

Racing boats

Sailboat racing varies from little dinghies hardly larger than surfboards to huge oceangoing vessels. One of the biggest events is the America's Cup, a race between just two boats. In 2010 the BMW Oracle team from San Francisco, CA, won the cup in this trimaran sailboat.

Surfing

Thrill seekers began riding wave crests on a piece of wood centuries ago in the South Pacific. In the mid-1960s, surfing became a global competitive sport. Surfers paddle their boards out to sea, wait for a wave, then stand up and ride it into shore at high speed.

Types of surfboard

Most boards have a plastic-foam core covered with layers of fiberglass and resin.

BODY BOARD	BIG WAVE BOARD	LONG BOARD	SHORT BOARD	FISH BOARD	TOW BOARD	RETRO EGG BOARD

Steering the spray
Surfers aim to stay just ahead of the spray from the breaking wave. They move with the wave as it changes course toward the shore.

Long-distance racing

The Volvo (Round the World) Ocean Race

How often?	Every 3 years
Time taken	9 months; starts in October
Distance	almost 39,000 nautical miles
Start/finish	Spain/Ireland
Number of legs, or sections	9 or 10
Longest period at sea	20 days
Temperature range	23°F to 104°F (−5°C to 40°C)
Wind speeds	Over 60 mph (100 kph)
Wave heights	Up to 100 ft. (30 m)
Number of crew members	11
Number of sets of clothes, per person	2

In 1990, New Zealander Peter Blake and his crew won the Round the World trophy.

More here

Waves of Grace by Patrick Doherty
The Old Man and the Sea by Ernest Hemingway
We Didn't Mean to Go to Sea by Arthur Ransome

America's Cup **Abby Sunderland** triathlon **kayak** slalom skiing **scuba** swim fins **lifeguard**

Make sailors' knots, such as bowline, clove hitch, rolling hitch, figure of eight, reef knot, and sheet bend.

Visit a coastal hotspot where all kinds of water sports are taught and practiced, such as Virginia's Northern Neck (Chesapeake Bay area); Honolulu, Hawaii; San Diego, California; Long Island, New York; Fort Myers Beach, Florida.

aft: the back of a boat.

barreling: surfing in the hollow, tubelike part of a wave as its top curls up and over its base.

boom: a horizontal pole that extends from the bottom of a sailboat's mast.

bow: the front of a boat.

port: the left-hand side of a boat.

starboard: the right-hand side of a boat.

Treasure hunters
In 1954, this diver off the Scottish coast was searching for gold coins believed to be on a galleon that had sunk in 1588. His helmet, sealed onto a waterproof suit, was first invented in the 1840s and had changed little. An exhaust valve was incorporated into the helmet and was supplied with air by a pump at the surface.

Exploring the deep

Since the first pearl divers, people have wanted to explore the ocean and its mysteries, from amazing animals to sunken treasure. Today, unmanned ROVs (remotely operated underwater vehicles) can peer into nearly every deep place.

360s **BCE** — **Aristotle,** *of ancient Greece, described how simple diving bells, or "cauldrons," worked.*

1620s — **Cornelius Drebbel** *built the first submarines and showed them off in the River Thames, London, even giving King James I a ride.*

1825 — **William James** *came up with a simple type of SCUBA (self-contained underwater breathing apparatus).*

1830s — **Augustus Siebe** *developed early types of diving helmets, and, by 1837, a complete diving suit.*

1867 — ***Ictineo II,*** *the first submarine not powered by humans, dived to 100 feet (30 m) for two hours.*

1934 — **Otis Barton** *and* **William Beebe** *dived to 3,028 feet (923 m).*

Bathysphere
Barton and Beebe's ball-shaped design resisted underwater pressure well.

1943 — **Jacques Cousteau** *invented the lightweight "aqualung" type of scuba still in use today.*

1960 — **Jacques Piccard** *and* **Don Walsh** *dived to a record depth of 35,797 feet (10,911 m) in the bathyscaphe* Trieste.

1977 — ***Alvin,*** *the famous submersible, located black smokers—deep-sea hydrothermal vents in the Pacific.*

1987 — **Craig Smith** *in* Alvin *was the first to observe a "whale fall"—rotting whale carcasses on the seabed.*

Submersible [*Shinkai 6500*]

A submersible is a small underwater research vessel designed for short trips. The Japanese-built *Shinkai 6500* is one of the best, diving down to a bone-crushing 21,325 feet (6,500 m). It gathers information in the immense depths and brings back samples of water, animal life, rocks, and seabed ooze.

Small space
Two pilots and a researcher squeeze into a space just 6.5 feet (2 m) wide.

Current meter
Records speed and direction of water flow.

Navigation sensor
Underwater sensors and a computerized navigation system fix exact location.

Horizontal thruster
This allows the craft to swivel, or turn, left or right.

Searchlights
Lights with a range of 33 feet (10 m) illuminate the ocean floor.

Stage one
Vessel is lowered into water by a support ship.

Stage two
Ballast tank takes on water and vessel begins descent.

TV and still cameras
These are used to record discoveries.

View port
The crew can view the ocean depths from this.

Stage three
Part of ballast weight is released to slow descent.

Stage four
Vessel descends slowly to seabed, using thrusters.

Sample basket
Holds tools and stores samples to bring back up.

Ballast tank
This tank is filled with seawater to go down, which is replaced with compressed air to come back up.

Rear thruster
A motorized propeller moves the vessel forward.

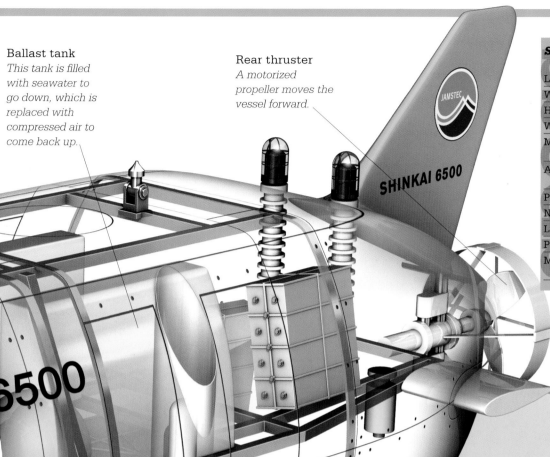

SHINKAI 6500

6500

Shinkai 6500 specifications

Length	31 ft. (9 m)
Width	9 ft. (2.7 m)
Height	10 ft. (3.2 m)
Weight on surface	29.4 tons
Maximum operation depth	21,325 ft. (6,500 m)
Accommodation	3 (2 pilots, 1 researcher)
Pressure hull diameter	6.5 ft. (2 m)
Normal dive duration	8 hours
Life support duration	129 hours
Payload	331 lbs. (150 kg) on surface
Maximum speed	2.5 knots (2.8 mph/4.6 kph)

Stage eight
Vehicle surfaces and is recovered by support ship.

Stages six and seven
Once research is done, water is expelled from the dive tank, remaining weight is thrown out, and the vessel begins its ascent.

Main battery
A rechargeable battery provides the power.

Pressure hull
Made from a very strong metal, the hull can withstand sea pressure.

Vertical thruster
This thruster makes small up-and-down adjustments to craft's position.

Stage five
Small dive trim tanks adjust so craft can cruise, settle, observe, and collect.

Ups and downs
Shinkai 6500 can stay under for eight hours. It dives and comes back up at around 131 feet (40 m) a minute. So it takes 2.5 hours to reach its deepest point and the same to return, leaving less than three hours for research work on the bottom.

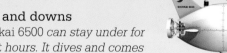

Rich_s from th_ s__. [Today's

The most valuable natural resource we get from the ocean today is crude oil, which can be found beneath the seabed. Its products, such as gasoline, diesel, fuel oils, and jet fuel, power our modern way of life.

Floating drill platform
This platform, or rig, houses drills that bore holes into the seabed, checking the amount and quality of oil in new wells.

Finding deep-sea oil

As oil from oil fields under land and shallow water is used up, oil companies explore deeper waters. Far out to sea are whole cities of drill rigs, production platforms, storage and processing ships, supply boats, helicopter pads, and "flotels" (floating hotels) for workers, all connected by thousands of miles of pipes and cables.

Under the floating Perdido drill platform in the Gulf of Mexico, the seabed is (2,450 m)

8,035 ft.

deep—six Empire State Buildings stacked one on top of the other

Umbilicals
These cables, wires, and tubes carry electricity, telephone lines, and computer communications.

Seabed transfer pipes
Crude oil straight from the wells is pumped through pipes that lie on the seafloor to the risers.

Drill bit
The drill bit grinds its way through rock, powered by the drill string. The drilling mud (a mix of watery fluids) flows via a hose to the top of the drill string, down through the string, out around the teeth of the bit, then back up between the drill string and its casing.

Rising oil
Natural pressure deep in the Earth may push the oil up, or the oil can be pumped.

Turning teeth
The drill bit has three sets of teeth that turn one another as they drill.

Drill string
The weight of the drill string sections pushes the drill bit into the rock.

OIL FIELD 18,000 FT. (5,500 M) DOWN

reasures]

FPSO ship
Crude oil arrives at the huge floating production, storage, and off-loading (FPSO) ship.

Processing
The oil is partly processed, or separated into components such as gasoline, and stored until it is off-loaded into visiting tankers.

Ocean minerals

Salt	85 million tons a year are collected by seawater evaporation
Gold	Nearly 22 million tons are dissolved in the oceans, but there is no easy way to extract it (yet)
Diamonds	Namibia, in Africa, mines more diamonds offshore than on land
Sand	Used to make concrete, bricks, and glass
Tin	Taken from the ocean floor; many uses

Mooring lines
Strong adjustable cables anchored to the seabed keep the platform and ship "on station" (in position), safe and stable during storms.

Risers
Crude oil flows up these pipes to the FPSO ship. The riser has a swivel joint or turret at the top so the FPSO can swing around with changing wind and wave direction.

Off-load supply lines
Crude oil or its fractions, or separate ingredients, flow through these lines to the off-loading dock.

Dock (off-load buoy)
Visiting tanker vessels attach to the dock to take on oil or its fractions from the FPSO ship.

Wellheads and pumping stations
The pumps keep the oil flowing from the wells through transfer pipes to the risers.

Rock layers
Oil and natural gas collect beneath impervious layers, which don't allow liquid or gas to pass through.

Sea beauties
For thousands of years, people have prized beautiful objects and materials made by sea creatures. Modern methods, such as culturing (farming) shellfish for pearls, save the animals in their natural habitats.

Ammonite fossils
These curly shelled cousins of squid died out with the dinosaurs.

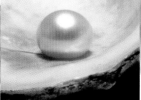

Pearls
Oysters cover a grain of sand with shell lining to make pearls.

Mother-of-pearl
This rainbow-colored shiny material lines some shells.

Harvesting the sea

The sea has provided humans with food for centuries, but, primarily because of overfishing, an estimated one-third of all ocean fish stocks has collapsed since 1900. Cod, salmon, anchovies (shown here), sharks, and more are in decline. Urgent global efforts could reverse this trend while protecting the age-old livelihood of fishing.

Pirates [Not just Caribbean]

Romantic tales describe brave pirates sailing the seas in search of buried treasure. But real life was very different. Pirates were criminals of the seas. Their world was full of hardship, robbery, violence, cruelty, and the torture and killing of innocent people. Many pirates were foul-mouthed bullies who ruled by terror. Probably only one, "Captain" Kidd, actually buried treasure for safekeeping.

Global pirates

Many pirates came from Britain, but pirates from China, India, and Turkey terrorized the eastern seas. In the Ukraine from the 16th to the 18th century, runaway servants and slaves formed a pirate republic and menaced cargo vessels on the Black Sea.

William "Captain" Kidd
Kidd began as a British privateer—a person authorized by the government to attack the ships and ports of an enemy nation. He turned to raiding the Atlantic and Indian Oceans, but was captured, tried, and hanged in London in 1701.

"Black Sam" Bellamy
Bellamy terrorized the waters off the Eastern Seaboard (east coast of North America). He captured more than 45 ships in less than two years but was said to be kind to his prisoners. He died in 1717 in a shipwreck off the coast of Massachusetts when he was just 28.

North America

CAPTAIN KIDD
EASTERN SEABOARD

BLACK SAM
EASTERN SEABOARD

BLACKBEARD
EASTERN SEABOARD, WEST INDIES

CHARLES VANE
BAHAMAS

Florida

Bahamas

West Indies

Caribbean Sea

Jamaica

CALICO JACK
BAHAMAS, BERMUDA, JAMAICA, EASTERN CARIBBEAN

Cutlass
This was a pirate's favorite weapon. It was normally used to cut ropes and slice sails.

Charles Vane
Working from the Bahamas, Vane had his own fleet, led by his powerful flagship Ranger. He was famous not just for killing enemies and prisoners but also for attacking other pirates and cutting them up. He was finally tried and hanged in Jamaica in 1721.

Anne Bonny and Mary Read

Both Bonny and Read came from poor families. For different reasons they dressed as boys when young. They teamed up with Calico Jack and were the only famous female pirates.

Atlantic Ocean

Treasure

Gold doubloons and pieces of eight (Spanish coins), precious jewels and gems, statues, paintings, and other works of art—all were taken by pirates, mainly in the Caribbean, to sell for food, rum, and ships' supplies. Pirates also stole cargoes of tea, molasses, whiskey, and rum, both to sell and for their own use.

Edward "Blackbeard" Teach

Teach wore his hair and beard long, sometimes decorated with colored ribbons, and on occasion he even lit slow-burning fuses in them. With his pistol belts and great boots, he could scare enemies simply with his appearance. He captured ships from Virginia to the West Indies, was pardoned once, and died fighting in 1718.

ANNE BONNY AND MARY READ
BAHAMAS, BERMUDA, JAMAICA, EASTERN CARIBBEAN

John "Calico Jack" Rackham

With Anne Bonny as his partner and Mary Read in his crew, Rackham attacked dozens of ships over a wide area. He was eventually caught by famous pirate hunter Jonathan Barnet, and was hanged in Jamaica in 1720.

Pirate timeline

Pirates have been around almost since seafaring began. Their "Golden Age" was between about 1600 and 1750, in the Caribbean and West Indies. They were active around the same time in the East Indies (South and Southeast Asia), taking prizes of spices and herbs.

75 BCE — **Julius Caesar,** *of ancient Rome, was held for ransom near Greece.*

750s–1100s CE — **Vikings** *from Scandinavia raided many areas, from North America to England to the Mediterranean.*

EARLY 1500s — **Barbarossa brothers** *Aruj and Hizir attacked Italian and Spanish ships in the Mediterranean many times. Aruj was killed in 1518, but Hizir ended up as Sultan of Algiers.*

1570s — **Francis Drake** *began his long career as explorer, slave trader, war captain, and, in the eyes of England's enemies, pirate.*

1600s — **Henry Morgan** *was one of the early pirates in the Spanish Main (Caribbean and Gulf of Mexico).*

1650s — **Mediterranean piracy** *began to fade as powerful nations sent naval fleets to restore law at sea and make the oceans safer places.*

1700 — **The Jolly Roger** *skull-and-crossbones pirate flag, its design attributed to Captain Emanuel Wynn, came into widespread use.*

1850s — **Piracy faded** *from South and Southeast Asia, 40 years after disappearing in the Caribbean.*

2000s — **Somali pirates** *off the coasts of northeast Africa capture oil tankers and people for ransom.*

Pirates today
Somali pirate leader Abdul Hassan commands 350 men.

Ocean legends [Tall tales]

After days at sea, thirsty and hungry and tired, a sailor begins to imagine things. What's that eerie noise and that shape in the mist? Since ancient times, sailors have told tales of sea monsters, ghost ships, and spirits of the deep. Modern science has found no evidence for them—yet!

Myths and monsters

Female creatures such as sirens and mermaids featured in many myths. The beautiful, part-bird sirens sang haunting songs to lure ships onto rocks, although these sounds may have been whale song. To explain sudden waves, winds, and storms, sailors invented huge monsters such as the giant, squidlike kraken and fire-breathing sea serpents.

Mermaids
Part women, part fish, mermaids were usually thought of as a bad omen, foretelling storms or wreckage. In stories and songs, they often used their beauty to lure sailors to a watery grave.

Killer from the deep
In 20,000 Leagues Under the Sea (background), the submarine crew battles with a huge, tentacled killer. Such monsters were probably based on real-life giant squid, which can grow to 49 feet (15 m) long.

Shipwrecker
Japanese legends feature the massive Umibozu, a shaven-headed, monklike spirit who took revenge on any ships that disturbed him.

Great sea gods
Ancient Roman sailors prayed for safe journeys to the sea god Neptune, who rode a chariot pulled by sea horses. The Greek sea god was Poseidon.

Mysteries

There are several stories about the sea that no one can quite explain. The following examples remain mysteries to this day.

Lost city of Atlantis

An earthquake may have destroyed and sunk the island of Atlantis, giving rise to the undersea legend.

The mystery of the *Marie Celeste*

In December 1872, this sailing ship was found drifting in the mid-Atlantic. She had left New York in November, bound for Genoa, Italy. There was no crew on board but no signs of trouble. No crewman was ever seen again.

Superstitions

To keep evil and bad luck at sea away, seagoing people have developed beliefs and habits.

Eyes

Around the world, eyes painted on boats are thought to scare away evil spirits.

Albatross

The souls of dead seafarers are supposed to live on in these large seabirds, so they must never be harmed or killed.

Dragons

Some Chinese sailors believe that dragons will keep away evil at sea as well as on land.

Bad bananas

Several lost ships in the 1700s carried bananas. The fruit has been considered bad luck ever since.

More here

20,000 Leagues Under the Sea
by Jules Verne
Moby-Dick
by Herman Melville
The Kraken Wakes
by John Wyndham

Bermuda triangle **giant squid** Leviathan **Charybdis** Kappa **Nereids**

Mystic Seaport, in Connecticut, offers a view into the lives and superstitions of sailors in the past, including a collection of figureheads designed to promote the good fortune of the ships they adorned.

kraken: the name in northern Europe and Iceland for a sea monster that looks like a huge octopus or squid.

league: an old measure of distance, slightly more than 3.25 miles (5.2 km).

Kamohoali'i: a shark god of Hawaii, one of many gods and spirits in the forms of fish and other sea creatures who feature in island folklore.

The ironclads
In 1862, in Hampton Roads, Virginia, during the Civil War, the CSS Virginia *(formerly the* Merrimac*) and the USS* Monitor *locked in battle, the first clash between two ironclad ships. The battle was inconclusive, but had huge significance. Around the world, naval powers halted the building of wooden-hulled ships.*

Waging war on water

Great battles on the oceans have often changed world history. Whoever ruled the seas also controlled trade routes and became rich and powerful. The last big sea conflicts were fought during World War II (1939–45); after that, air forces took over.

480 BCE — **Salamis** *380 Greek ships took on 1,200 Persian ships, and won.*

31 BCE — **Actium** *More than 550 Egyptian and Roman ships fought in the Ionian Sea. Rome won and an empire was born.*

1279 — **Yamen, China** *The Mongol-led Yuan dynasty of Kublai Khan destroyed more than 1,000 ships of the Song dynasty, ending Song rule across much of East Asia.*

1571 — **Lepanto, Greece** *A coalition of Catholic maritime states defeated a huge fleet of the Ottoman Empire.*

1588 — **Spanish Armada** *A Spanish force of 130 ships was damaged by the English fleet, then forced north, where it was destroyed by gales.*

1776 — **Long Island** *The first big sea battle of the Revolutionary War was lost by the inexperienced American forces.*

1805 — **Trafalgar** *The British fleet under Lord Horatio Nelson conquered combined French and Spanish forces off Spain during the Napoleonic Wars.*

1916 — **Jutland** *The biggest-ever sea conflict in ship sizes and numbers. The British and German navies fought near Denmark in World War I.*

1942 — **Midway** *The most important conflict in the Pacific in World War II, between US and Japanese forces.*

1944 — **Leyte Gulf** *The last great sea battle of World War II, between the Allies and Japan in the Philippines. More ships were sunk than ever before.*

1950 — **Inchon** *A Korean War sea battle won by the United Nations. It led to the recapture of the South Korean capital, Seoul.*

Tsunamis | Dangerous oceans

Tsunamis are giant ocean waves caused by undersea earthquakes, volcanic eruptions, mudslides, rockfalls, and similar sudden, enormous Earth movements. Throughout history, they have brought death and destruction without warning to coastal cities and peoples around the world.

พื้นที่เสี่ยงภัยคลื่นยักษ์
TSUNAMI HAZARD ZONE

IN CASE OF EARTHQUAKE, GO TO HIGH GROUND OR INLAND
เมื่อเกิดแผ่นดินไหว ให้หนีห่าง
จากชายหาดและขึ้นที่สูงโดยเร็ว

Warning signs
International signs show people that an area is at risk of tsunamis, how much time they have, and how they should escape. Warnings are also sent via TV, radio, the Internet, and text messages.

Waves of destruction

c.1600 BCE
The Mediterranean island of Santorini (Thera) blew up. A resulting 100-m (330-ft) tsunami devastated the Minoan civilization of Crete and may have started the legend of the lost city of Atlantis.

NOVEMBER 1755
A powerful earthquake and tsunami, followed by fires, destroyed Lisbon, Portugal. More than 60,000 people died.

AUGUST 1883
In Southeast Asia, Krakatoa volcano exploded. A 40-m (130-ft) tsunami drowned more than 35,000 people.

DECEMBER 1908
An earthquake between Italy and Sicily resulted in a 12-m (39-ft) tsunami with a death toll of 150,000.

APRIL 1946
An Alaskan quake's tsunami travelled as far south as Hawaii, killing 160. The Pacific Tsunami Warning System was set up in 1949.

JULY 1958
The tallest tsunami ever followed another Alaskan quake. The waves funnelled into an inlet and grew to over 500 m (1,640 ft), higher than the Empire State Building! Due to the remote location, only two fishermen died.

MAY 1960
In Chile, the strongest-ever recorded quake and its tsunami killed 5,000 people.

AUGUST 1976
One of the worst Philippines tsunamis resulted in 7,000 deaths.

DECEMBER 2004
The Indian Ocean tsunami followed a 9.3-magnitude earthquake west of Sumatra. More than 230,000 people died.

MARCH 2011
A huge undersea quake near Japan sent 35-m (115-ft) tsunamis onto the northeast coast. 23,700 died or were declared missing.

Story of a tsunami

The biggest tsunamis are usually due to earthquakes or eruptions that move great areas of rock, either under the ocean or next to it. This movement causes pressure waves in the water, which ripple outward in all directions for hundreds of miles.

1. Earth movements
One part of the seabed, called a plate, slips down against another plate, giving the water a giant push.

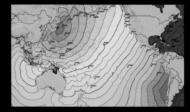

2. Spreading out
The pressure wave spreads through the ocean at up to 500 mph (800 kph), losing strength from red to blue.

3. At the coast
The pressure wave reaches the shallows, sucks water down the beach, rears up to a great height, and surges inland.

Tohoku earthquake and tsunami
This double disaster hit northeast Japan on March 11, 2011. A gigantic earthquake 42 miles (70 km) out at sea shook the land. It also generated a massive series of waves that swept 6 miles (10 km) inland. Buildings, bridges, roads, and railways were washed away, and vast areas of farmland were destroyed. Almost half a million people were made homeless.

Wrecked! [The *Titanic*]

TITANIC STEWARD'S BADGE

Across the world's oceans, sunken ships sleep on the seabed. Old wooden ones may not last long, but metal ships stay around for centuries. Some still hold the remains of people and are regarded as graves, to be treated with great respect. One of the most famous wrecks is that of the *Titanic*, which sank in 1912.

World class

The *Titanic* was the largest passenger liner in the world, able to carry more than 3,500 people. She was designed using some of the most advanced technologies of the time and was the pride of her owner, the White Star Line.

Unsinkable
The Titanic *set sail from Southampton for New York on April 10, on her maiden voyage. She was believed to be unsinkable but had advanced safety features just in case!*

Floating palace
The ship was the height of luxury. In first class there was a swimming pool, restaurants, and gyms, and there were barbers and libraries for both first and second class. Even third class was stylish and comfortable.

Rich and famous
Many prominent people from both sides of the Atlantic signed on for the maiden voyage. Millionaires John Jacob Astor IV and Benjamin Guggenheim would have swept down this staircase.

Life preservers
The ship carried 3,500 life preservers, but they were no use in the icy seas (28°F, −2°C) of the Atlantic; people died of hypothermia within 15 minutes.

Going down

At night on April 14 in calm seas, the *Titanic* hit a massive iceberg. Within 30 minutes the ship was listing badly and Captain Edward J. Smith ordered the lowering of the lifeboats. Just under three hours after the collision, the "unsinkable" *Titanic* sank. 1,513 people were lost.

Scandal
The evacuation was badly mismanaged. The ship carried 20 lifeboats with a capacity of 1,178 people, but only about 700 boarded the boats.

And the band played on . . .
Titanic's heroic band continued to play until she sank below the waves.

Searching the seas

Ever since the *Titanic* sank, attempts were made to find her. In September 1985, a joint US-French expedition, led by Jean-Louis Michel and Dr. Robert Ballard, succeeded in locating the wreckage.

Alvin
In 1986, the first manned dives to the wreck were undertaken in the submersible Alvin. The wreck was 2.5 miles (4 km) down.

The operation underway
In 1985, the French ship Le Suroit, with deep-search sonar, and the US ship Knorr began the search. Titanic was found only 13 miles (21 km) from the last position given by her fourth officer in 1912.

Discovery
Researchers assumed that the ship had sunk in one piece, but the search team found that she had split apart, the bow (above) lying 1,970 feet (600 m) from the stern.

Other shipwrecks

Shipwrecks have happened for centuries, often in war, sometimes due to weather, and occasionally due to human error.

1400 BCE — *The earliest known wreck with treasure sank near Uluburun, off the coast of Turkey. She was found intact in 1982.*

1120s –1270s CE — ***Nanhai No. 1*** *This huge Chinese merchant ship sank holding 80,000 items. She is now raised and displayed.*

1535 — *The earliest known wreck in the New World was a Spanish ship laden with treasure, which sank off Hispaniola on the way home.*

1545 — ***Mary Rose*** *This flagship of English king Henry VIII sank near the Isle of Wight, southern England. She is now raised and displayed in Portsmouth, where she was built.*

1628 — ***Vasa*** *This Swedish navy ship sank minutes into her first voyage. She had not been ready to sail, but the king wanted her to join his Baltic fleet. She is now raised and displayed in Stockholm.*

1850 — ***Ayrshire*** *This British emigrant ship ran aground off New Jersey. A "life car," a boat hauled between the shore and the wreck on ropes, rescued all the passengers and crew except one.*

1915 — ***Lusitania*** *This British passenger ship was sunk near Ireland by a German submarine, bringing the United States into World War I. 1,198 died.*

1941 — ***Bismarck*** *The biggest German battleship of its time was sunk by the British navy in the Atlantic.*

1987 — ***Dõna Paz*** *The official death toll from this Philippine ferry disaster was 1,749, but the vessel was so overcrowded that more than 4,000 may have died.*

2002 — ***Le Joola*** *This Senegalese ferry capsized off the Gambian coast. She was designed to carry 580 people, but around 2,000 were on board. At least 1,863 people died.*

Oce
under

‿‿ Which city is in immediate danger from the sea?

* How do cruise ships add to a garbage patch?

‿‿ How does your favorite sandwich endanger fish?

ans
threat

Pollution [Ocean trash can?]

Not so long ago, people dumped sewage and trash into the sea and forgot about them. But today there are too many people—and too much long-lasting refuse—to keep using the oceans as a global garbage can.

Currents and tides

Floating items can travel thousands of miles with currents and tides. Instead of spreading them out, currents may bring them together as dirty "rafts" of stinking garbage that wash up on beaches and shores.

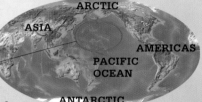

North Pacific Gyre
This gigantic clockwise ocean current sweeps trash from its edges around and inward.

Great Pacific Garbage Patch
A huge area in the North Pacific, 1,560 miles (2,500 km) across, is a floating trash dump. Most of this garbage is tiny pieces of plastic.

Oil spills

Oil leaks and blowouts on land are difficult to control. At sea, the source of the leak may be on the dark, deep seabed and even more difficult to "cap." Strong water currents continually carry away the thick goo, causing terrible damage far and wide.

Oil spill disasters, by tons of oil spilled

Middle East Gulf conflict, 1991	Up to 250,000,000
Lakeview oil field, California, 1910	1,200,000
Deepwater Horizon, Gulf of Mexico, 2010	713,922
Ixtoc 1 drill rig, Gulf of Mexico, 1979	470,000
Atlantic Empress tanker, Trinidad, 1979	285,000
Fergana Valley oil field, Uzbekistan, 1992	280,000
Nowruz platform, Persian Gulf, 1983	260,000

Cleaning up

Cleanup operations must start fast, before the oil spreads too much. But the Ixtoc I oil well blowout in the southern Gulf of Mexico continued for ten months and did untold damage to fisheries, coasts, and wildlife. In Alaska, oil that leaked from the tanker Exxon Valdez in 1989 still causes damage today.

Where's it from?

Up to 80 percent of ocean pollution comes from the land—city sewage and trash, farming pesticides and fertilizers, and waste from the food and chemical industries. The rest is mainly plastics, fishing nets, oil platform debris, and general ship and boat waste.

Cruise ships
A 3,000-passenger cruise ship produces more than 1 ton of solid waste each day.

Farming
Fertilizers are washed along streams and rivers to the sea. They encourage plankton to grow too fast, and they form toxic tides.

Plastics
Bags, bottles, nets, ropes, and floats take years to decompose (break down). Some animals think they are food, eat them, and die.

An oily end
Animals, plants, shoreline rocks, and beaches are all affected by an oil spill. Whales and dolphins suffer clogged blowholes and cannot breathe. Birds try to clean their clogged feathers, swallow the oil, and suffer a slow, painful death.

More here

Tracking Trash: Flotsam, Jetsam, and the Science of Ocean Motion by Loree Griffin Burns
The Iron Woman by Ted Hughes

Exxon Valdez **Deepwater Horizon** NOAA **Jacques Cousteau** 5 Gyres Institute

Practice safe and clean boating: Do not dispose of trash or toilet waste in the ocean, and use environmentally friendly cleaning agents and boat paint.

Don't try to rescue pollution-affected or shore-stranded animals like birds and seals. Instead, tell the local police or coast guard.

pesticide: a chemical used for killing pests, especially insects and rodents.

biodegradable: capable of being broken down naturally by the action of worms, molds, and other living things and returned safely to the soil or water. Most plastics are not biodegradable.

Exp nding oce ns [Higher

Slowly, the level of our oceans is rising. There has been an increase of 0.08 inches (2 mm) each year over the past 100 years, and this rate will speed up. By 2100, the ocean surface could be 20 inches (0.5 m) higher, flooding cities and vast farming areas. Scientists believe this increase is caused by global warming.

What is global warming?

We use huge amounts of energy obtained by burning fuels such as oil, coal, and gas. The burning releases gases—especially carbon dioxide, or CO_2—that trap heat in the atmosphere through the "greenhouse effect." The extra heat is warming up our planet, causing ice caps and glaciers to melt as the climate changes.

SUN'S HEAT AND LIGHT RAYS

Greenhouse effect
The Sun's heat passes into the atmosphere and warms it, the oceans, and the land. With rising amounts of greenhouse gases, more of the heat is held in the atmosphere, and less can go out into space.

EXTRA HEAT IS UNABLE TO ESCAPE

Earth's atmosphere
In addition to CO_2, other increasing greenhouse gases include methane, from animal digestion, and ozone, from car exhaust.

EARTH

Melting ice on land

Global warming means the world's main ice sheets on land—on Antarctica, Greenland, and around the Arctic Circle—are gradually melting. The water runs into seas and oceans, making their levels rise.

Greenland
The area of ice that melts during Greenland's summer increased by one-sixth in just ten years.

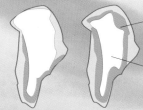

GREENLAND, 1992 **GREENLAND, 2002**

Melted ice
Orange shows the area of ice sheet that melts in summer.

Still ice
White shows the permanent ice remaining during summer.

Rising sea levels

As icebergs and floating ice sheets melt, they do not add to the rise in sea levels, since they are already in seas and oceans. Part of the rise is water from melted ice on land, and seawater itself increases in volume as it gets warmer.

Venice in trouble
This low-lying lagoon city in Italy is already in trouble as waves lap higher each year.

RISE OF 3 FT./1 M

Amsterdam
A major port, the capital of the Netherlands would flood with a rise of just 6 feet (2 m).

RISE OF 6 FT./2 M

San Francisco
With a rise of 10 feet (3 m), this "City by the Bay" would begin to disappear.

RISE OF 10 FT./3 M

London
Large areas of South London, England, would be covered by a rise of 15 feet (4.5 m).

RISE OF 15 FT./4.5 M

Shanghai
In China, the world's biggest, busiest port could have ships in its city streets if the sea level went up by 20 feet (6 m).

RISE OF 20 FT./6 M

The Arctic Ocean may have its first ice-free summer by

2040,

or maybe 2039, or 2038 . . .

Liberty drowning
If all the main ice sheets in the Antarctic and Arctic melted (including those on Greenland), sea levels would increase by more than 230 feet (70 m). That is enough to reach the shoulders of New York's famous Statue of Liberty!

Threatened species [Help!]

Right now, in all the world's oceans, creatures are at risk of becoming extinct (dying out forever). Many people are unaware of the huge problems, partly because sea animals and the dangers they face are hidden beneath the waves. Threats vary greatly, from pollution and global warming to being caught accidentally in fishing nets or on purpose for our dinner tables.

How threatened?

For each species, experts need information: How many are there? How widely are they spread? How fast do they breed? They also need to know the dangers they face, such as loss of food or habitats.

Vulnerable
In this group are animals that are not in immediate danger—but they could be in coming years. We need to take early action to protect them and their habitats.

MANATEE

Endangered
These animals are already in serious trouble. Without our urgent help, their numbers will continue to fall until they no longer exist.

GALÁPAGOS FUR SEAL

Critically endangered
Creatures in this most serious category are staring extinction in the face. Without drastic action now, they will not make it. They could be gone in 30 years or even sooner.

LEATHERBACK TURTLE

Threats from humans

Beluga whale	Pollution, boat disturbance, hunting in some areas
Blue whale	Boat strikes, tangling in fishing gear
Humpback whale	Boat strikes, illegal hunting
Killer whale	Loss of food, pollution, oil spills, boat disturbance
Spotted seal	Melting sea ice, hunting for skins
Leatherback turtle	Disturbed nests, pollution, eating floating garbage
Loggerhead turtle	Tangling in fishing gear
Bocaccio rockfish	Bycatch, changing ocean currents
Sockeye salmon	Diseases from salmon farms
Black abalone	Overfishing, diseases due to global warming
Elkhorn coral	Diseases made worse by warming waters
Staghorn coral	As above; also water clouded with sediments

Until the 1980s, ambergris, a secretion in sperm whales, was used in scents. Whales died so people could smell good!

More here

Miss L'eau by Theresa Katz

IUCN Red Lists
Census of Marine Life
endangered habitat loss
survival **overfishing**

Support beaches where marine conservation is a priority. "Adopt" a marine animal through a good program. Join an underwater cleanup group. If you go boating, watch out for marine life.

Don't buy seafood, such as tuna and shrimp, unless it is fished in a responsible way.

bycatch: animals caught accidentally, such as turtles, dolphins, or sharks trapped in nets intended for shoals of small fish.

sustainable: able to be maintained at a certain level, such as fish being caught in numbers that still allow them to reproduce and grow.

POLAR BEAR

GALÁPAGOS MARINE IGUANA

BLUE WHALE

GREEN TURTLE

STERN GRAY WHALE

CARIBBEAN ELECTRIC RAY

SMALLTOOTH SAWFISH

SOUTHERN BLUEFIN TUNA

Final frontier

We know more about the surface of the Moon than we know about our oceans. Oceans leave so much to be discovered and studied—winds, waves, wildlife, and deep-sea treasures. There's no better place for explorers in search of adventure.

Science at sea

Worldwide, thousands of scientists work in ships called RVs (research vessels). Others fly in spotter planes to track migrating whales, changing sandbars, and drifting currents. Below the surface, in addition to submersibles, there are undersea bases where people can live for days, using diving equipment to explore their surroundings.

Tags and tracking
Harmless electronic tags on sea creatures measure where they go and the surrounding water depth and temperature. The tags send information to satellites in space.

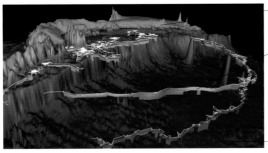

— *Antarctic peninsula*

— *In these tracks of elephant seal feeding trips, red shows their deepest dives.*

— *Southern Ocean*

Epic journeys
The tags allow scientists to record where an animal travels. Elephant seal tags show that they swim more than 620 miles (1,000 km) and dive down more than 7,550 feet (2,300 m) when feeding.

All in a day's work
It's exciting being an ocean scientist. There is work to do around the clock, like studying fish that come to the surface only at night. And new discoveries are helping us understand global warming, how to get energy from tides, and wave power.

Hitching a ride
Marine biologists are lifted back onto their research vessel with the samples they have collected.

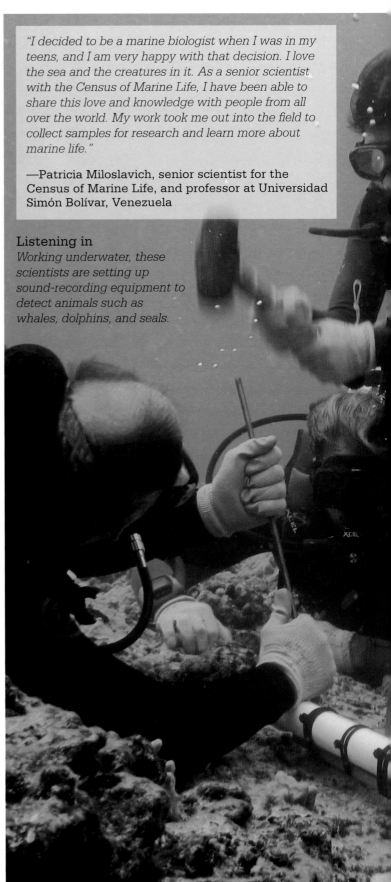

"I decided to be a marine biologist when I was in my teens, and I am very happy with that decision. I love the sea and the creatures in it. As a senior scientist with the Census of Marine Life, I have been able to share this love and knowledge with people from all over the world. My work took me out into the field to collect samples for research and learn more about marine life."

—Patricia Miloslavich, senior scientist for the Census of Marine Life, and professor at Universidad Simón Bolívar, Venezuela

Listening in
Working underwater, these scientists are setting up sound-recording equipment to detect animals such as whales, dolphins, and seals.

habitat]

Weird and wonderful

The Census of Marine Life (2000–2010) was a huge project to catalog what lives where in the oceans. It raised the number of known species from 230,000 to 250,000. Below are some animals discovered by the Census. The ocean scientists of tomorrow are sure to discover more amazing creatures like these.

YETI CRAB

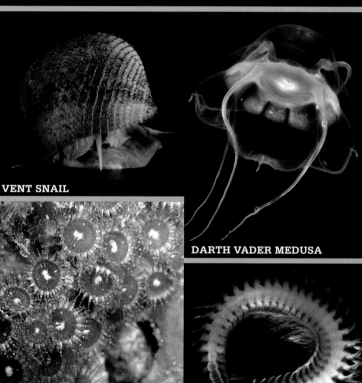

VENT SNAIL

DARTH VADER MEDUSA

NEW CORALS

DEAD-WHALE-EATING WORM

ISOPOD

More here

Virtual Apprentice: Oceanographer by Don Rauf and Monique Vescia
Science 101: Ocean Science by Jennifer Hoffman

Census of Marine Life marine biologist **ecology** Mariana Trench **marine biodiversity**

Be amazed by photos and videos of just-discovered ocean creatures:
• http://www.coml.org/image-gallery
• http://www.coml.org/video-gallery

Visit the Virginia Aquarium and Marine Science Center in Virginia Beach. Sign up for the animal encounters program at the Vancouver Aquarium, British Columbia, Canada.

biological oceanographers: scientists who study all forms of life in the oceans.

marine chemists: experts who analyze the chemical makeup of seawater and seafloor sediments.

marine geologists: scientists who map the mountains and valleys of the seafloor.

physical oceanographers: experts who study the movement of the oceans.

Future oceans

Over many years, we have seriously harmed parts of the oceans and their wildlife, yet some areas remain almost untouched, packed and thriving with amazing features and incredible animals. Because all the oceans are vital to life, it's time for people everywhere to care for and celebrate Earth's wonderful oceans and the plants and animals that live in them.

Oc an favorit s [Superstars]

Small fish and seabed worms can be fascinating, but bigger, bolder, and more captivating creatures command our attention. The animals shown here play very important roles in their habitats. Not all are under threat, but they show us how ocean life is coping with today's hazards.

Sea turtles

Group	Reptiles
Number of species	7
Range	Migratory; mostly warmer waters
Breeding	Lay eggs in sand
Typical lifespan	50–75 years
Status	All species are under serious threat and are protected
Threats	Pollution, disturbed breeding beaches and eggs, hunting

Hawksbill turtle
Hunted for its shell, it is now critically endangered.

Penguins

Group	Birds
Number of species	17–20 (debated)
Range	South of the Equator, mostly around Antarctica
Breeding	Lay eggs
Typical lifespan	15–20 years
Status	6 species are endangered
Threats	Global warming, fishing boats and nets, lack of food due to humans fishing

Adélie penguins
These penguins use the Sun to find their way across the ice.

Chinstrap penguin
These may swim more than 50 miles (80 km) from land when feeding.

African penguins
This is the only penguin species that breeds in Africa.

Sharks

Group	Fish
Number of species	About 440
Range	All waters, even polar
Breeding	Most lay eggs; some give birth to pups
Typical lifespan	A few years; up to 100 for the biggest
Status	Dozens are under threat
Threats	Fishing lines and nets, hunting, pollution

Great white shark
Despite the myths, humans are not this shark's preferred prey.

Lemon shark
This tropical inshore shark eats fish, including stingrays.

Scalloped hammerhead
The hammerlike head may help this shark see and smell prey.

Whales

Group	Mammals
Number of species	15 baleen, 75 toothed (includes dolphins)
Range	All waters, even polar
Breeding	Give birth to calves
Typical lifespan	20 to 130-plus
Status	Dozens are threatened, some critically endangered
Threats	Fishing lines and nets, hunting, collisions with boats, chemical and noise pollution

Narwhal
This northern toothed whale has only two teeth; one grows into a 10-foot (3 m) tusk.

Sperm whale
The world's biggest predator, a large bull, or male, is 65 feet (20 m) long and weighs 60-plus tons.

Young olive ridley turtle

One of the smallest sea turtles, the adult has a shell about 2 feet (60 cm) long.

Leatherback turtle

The biggest of all turtles, it weighs up to 2,000 pounds (900 kg), with front flippers nearly 10 feet (3 m) across.

Leatherback turtle eggs

Females can lay eight separate clutches (sets), with 100 eggs in each.

Macaroni penguin

These birds form huge, crowded breeding colonies of more than 150,000.

Gentoo penguin chick

By three months old, this youngster will be feeding on krill, fish, and squid, far out at sea.

Rockhopper penguin

These got their name because they hop from rock to rock.

Whale shark

This enormous fish, at almost 40 feet (12 m) long, is a harmless plankton feeder.

Tiger shark

Although considered dangerous to humans, the attack rate of this shark is actually surprisingly low.

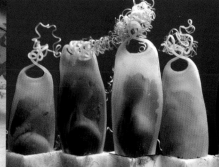

Shark eggs

Baby sharks develop over several months in protective egg cases.

Humpback mother and calf

Like other mammals, the humpback feeds its young milk, in this case for up to 10 months.

Minke whale

This is one of the smallest baleen whales, at 33 feet (10 m) long and 12–14 tons in weight.

Bowhead

The bowhead has the longest baleen of any whale, at 10 feet (3 m), and weighs 80 tons.

Abyssal zone
The deepest, darkest zone in oceans and seas, below about 13,200 feet (4,000 m).

Algae
Simple plants that have no true roots or flowers. Most seaweeds are types of algae.

Armada
The Spanish word for a large gathering of ships and boats, usually for the purpose of attack or waging war.

Baleen
Long hairy or fringed pieces of cartilage hanging from the upper jaws of great whales, used to filter small food items from the water.

Bathysphere
A deep-sea underwater craft shaped like a ball or sphere.

Bay
An area of sea or ocean that is partly or mostly surrounded by land, often shaped like a C or U.

Bioluminescence
The light produced by living things through chemical processes.

Blubber
A layer of fatty substances below the skin that keeps cold out and body warmth in.

Break
The point at which the crest, or top, of a wave curls over and tumbles down onto its base.

Camouflage
To hide or stay unnoticed by blending in with the surroundings.

Cartilage
A rubbery substance, lightweight and slightly bendable, that makes up the skeletons of some creatures, such as sharks, skates, and rays.

Chlorophyll
The pigment, or green-colored substance, that plants use to catch light energy and change it into energy-rich food.

Clutch
A set of eggs all laid around the same time and in the same place.

Coalition
A group brought together for a common purpose, such as a group of nations joined to fight an enemy.

Colonial
Living together in a group or colony.

Condense
To change from a gas or vapor to a liquid—the reverse of evaporation. Invisible floating water vapor condenses to liquid water.

Container
A large, standard-size metal box used for storage that can be moved easily and stacked on ships.

Continent
Any of the seven largest landmasses on planet Earth (North America, South America, Europe, Asia, Africa, Australia, and Antarctica).

Continental shelf
The area around most main landmasses, which is flat and covered by water usually less than 490 feet (150 m) deep.

Crude oil
Liquid petroleum as it is found in the Earth before it is processed into various products.

Decompose
To rot or decay into seabed sediments or soil.

Denticle
A tiny toothlike scale on the skins of sharks, rays, and similar fish.

Dorsal
On the back or topmost surface, such as on the upper side of fish.

Ecosystem
A community of living things, such as plants and animals, as well as the surrounding rocks, soil, waters, and all other natural features.

Evaporate
To change from a liquid to a gas or vapor—the reverse of condensation. Liquid water evaporates to invisible floating water vapor.

Gasoline
A flammable (easily set on fire) liquid created by mixing natural gas and crude oil. Gasoline is used especially as a fuel for automobiles and other vehicles.

Gill
A frilly or feathery body part used for breathing underwater by many animals, such as fish, worms, crabs, and sea slugs.

Greenhouse gas
Gas in the atmosphere that increases the warming effect of the Sun on the Earth.

Gulf
A very large bay or inlet from a sea or ocean, such as the Gulf of Mexico.

Habitat
A particular type of living place or surroundings, such as a pond, desert, rocky seashore, reef, or deep seabed.

Holdfast
The rootlike part of some seaweeds that anchors them onto a base such as rock or wood.

Hormone
A natural chemical substance that animals or plants use to control body processes, especially growth.

Hypothermia
Very low body temperature, which can cause the illness or death of someone.

Impervious
Not allowing liquids or gases to pass through.

The oceans of the world contain more than 18 million tons of gold

Glossary

Invertebrate
An animal without a backbone or vertebral column.

Isopod
A small crustacean with seven pairs of legs. There are around 4,500 marine species of isopod.

Krill
Small shrimplike creatures, mostly smaller than a little finger, that are important parts of food chains and food webs in oceans and seas.

List
To lean or tilt to the side, perhaps at a dangerous angle.

Mammal
A warm-blooded animal whose newborn young feed on their mothers' milk. Most mammals have a body covering of hair or fur, but water mammals such as whales have only a little hair.

Mineral
A natural chemical substance that makes up rocks and that is broken down by weather and other processes.

Paralyze
To stop movement by preventing the muscles from working.

Parasitism
The relationship in which two kinds of living things live together closely and one, the parasite, causes harm to the other, the host, for its own benefit.

Peninsula
An area of land that is surrounded on most sides by water but is still joined to the mainland.

Pesticide
A chemical substance that harms or kills pests, usually farm pests such as insects or worms, or pests harmful to humans.

Photophore
A body part that gives out light in a living thing that is bioluminescent.

Phytoplankton
The plant subset of plankton. *See* plankton.

Plankton
Animals, plants, and other living things that drift in water rather than actively swim. Most are tiny but some, such as jellyfish, are large.

Plate (tectonic plate)
One of the huge pieces of hard rock that make up the Earth's crust, or outer shell.

Plateau
A large area that is mostly flat, usually with lower areas around it. There are plateaus on land and under seas and oceans.

Predator
An animal that catches and eats other animals.

Prey
An animal that is caught and eaten by other animals.

Quartz
A very common mineral, also called silica, that contains silicon and oxygen. It makes up many kinds of rocks, such as sandstone, and particles, such as sand.

Red List
A list showing the conservation status of species, prepared by the International Union for Conservation of Nature (IUCN).

ROV
Remotely Operated underwater Vehicle—a robot submersible controlled by an operator, usually on a nearby ship.

Scale
A small, rigid plate that grows out of an animal's skin, protecting it from predators and climate. Scales are found on fish and reptiles, but they are also on some birds, insects, and mammals.

Scavenge
To feed on dead and dying animals and plants.

Sclerite
A hardened body part. Sclerites occur on some animals, including sponges and some corals.

Scuba
Self-Contained Underwater Breathing Apparatus (also known as Aqua-Lung)—a machine that allows people to swim freely underwater while breathing normally.

Sediment
Small particles such as gravel, sand, clay, silt, or mud that are swept along by water, wind, or ice and settle on the bottom of a body of water.

Skeleton
The strong parts or framework of an animal that give it shape and support. There are two different skeletal types: the exoskeleton, or stable outer shell, and the endoskeleton, the support structure inside the body.

Sodium chloride
The main salt or mineral dissolved in seawater. In a pure form, it is the table salt we use for cooking and putting on our food.

Species
A particular group of living thing, whose members look similar and breed together.

Strait
A narrow passage or channel of water between two areas of land, such as the Strait of Gibraltar or the Strait of Magellan.

Vertebrae
The backbones, or individual bones of the spine, in a skeleton.

Whale fall
The dead body of a whale that has sunk to the seabed. In deep water, the carcass can provide food for the animals in a local ecosystem for decades.

Zooplankton
The animal subset of plankton. *See* plankton.

Index

There are more than 230,000

marine species in the seas and oceans

PHOTOGRAPHY

1: iStockphoto; 2–3: NASA/Science Faction/Corbis; 6bl, 7l: Keith Ellenbogen/Blue Reef; 7cl, 7cr: Shutterstock; 7r: iStockphoto; 8–9: Keren Su/Corbis; 10–11: Norbert Wu/Getty Images; 12c: Shutterstock; 14tr: Zoonar GmbH/Alamy; 14mr: Pete Oxford/Getty Images; 14b: NASA Goddard Space Flight Center; 15tl: Ulof Bjorg Christianson/Rainbo/Science Faction/Corbis; 15tc, 15tr: Shutterstock; 15tml: Brian J. Skerry/National Geographic; 15tmc: Jens Kuhfs/Getty Images; 15tmr: Dante Fenolio/Photo Researchers; 15bml: Norbert Wu/Minden Pictures/National Geographic; 15bmc: David Shale/Nature Picture Library; 15bmr: David Shale/Nature Picture Library; 15bl: University of Aberdeen/Natural Environment Research Council; 15bc: NOAA; 15br: Monterey Bay Aquarium Research Institute; 18bl: WaterFrame/Alamy; 19tr: Bertrand Gardel/Hemis/Corbis; 20tl: Shutterstock; 20bl: National Geographic/Getty Images; 20br: B. Clarke/ClassicStock/The Image Works; 21bl: Tanya G Burnett/SeaPics; 21br: Stefan Feldhoff/A. C. Martin/dpa/Landov; 22cl: Dave Bartruff/Corbis; 22–23: Jonah Kessel/Moodboard/Corbis; 23tr: Sean Davey/Corbis; 24tmr, 24bmr: Shutterstock; 24tl, 24tr, 24–25: Bryn Walls; Andrew J. Martinez/Science Photo Library/Photo Researchers; 25tl: Manfred Kage/Photo Researchers; 25bml: Kelly-Mooney Photography/Corbis; 25tr: Gallo Images/Duif du Toit/Getty Images; 25cr: Photolibrary/Getty Images; 25br: Stuart Morton/Getty Images; 26l: Scubazoo/Alamy; 26c: Popperfoto/Getty Images; 26r: Dorian Weisel/Corbis; 28tr: Shutterstock; 28bl: Scubazoo/Alamy; 28mr: Herwarth Voigtmann/Corbis; 28br: Bill Brooks/Alamy; 29tl, 29tcl, 29tcr, 29tr: Shutterstock; 28tml: MediaBakery; 28tmr: NASA; 28b: Arctic Photo; 30–31: Dorian Weisel/Corbis; 32tr, 32tc, 32c: iStockphoto; 32ml, 32bl: Sygma/Corbis; 33tl, 33tr, 33bmr: iStockphoto; 33tml: Paul Thompson/FPG/Getty Images; 33tmr, 33bml, 33bl: Shutterstock; 34mr: Shutterstock; 34bl: North Wind Picture Archives/Alamy; 34br: National Geographic/Getty Images; 34–35: iStockphoto; 35tl: Popperfoto/Getty Images; 35tr: SSPL/Getty Images; 35mr: Shutterstock; 35bl: AFP/Getty Images; 36l: Shutterstock; 36c: David Scharf/Science Faction/Corbis; 36r: Visuals Unlimited/Corbis; 38–39: Richard Herrmann/Galatee Films; 39t, 39tml, 39tmr, 39bml, 39bmr, 39bl, 39br: Shutterstock; 40tl, 40tmr, 40bcl: iStockphoto; 40tml: John Clegg/Photo Researchers, Inc.; 40bml: Richard Herrmann/SeaPics.com; 40tr: Roland Birke/Peter Arnold/Photolibrary; 40bmcl: Denis Scott/Corbis; 40bl, 40bmr: Shutterstock; 41tl: John Clegg/Photo Researchers; 41tc: iStockphoto; 41tr: Paul Nicklen/National Geographic/Corbis; 41tml: Harry Taylor/Getty Images; 41tmcr, 41bmcr, 41bml, 41bl, 41bcl: Shutterstock; 41br: Stephen Frink Collection/Alamy; 42–43, 42bml, 42bmr, 42bl, 42bcl, 42bcr, 42br: iStockphoto; 43tr: Arco Images GmbH/Alamy; 43mr: David Scharf/Corbis; 43br: David Scharf/Corbis; 44–45: Gerald Nowak/age footstock; 46ml, 46bmc, 46bl, 46bcl: Shutterstock; 46tr, 46bmcr, 46br: iStockphoto; 47c: Shutterstock; 47tr: National Geographic/Getty Images; 48–49: Fred Bavendum/Minden Pictures; 49tr: Norbert Wu/Getty Images; 49tmr: Visuals Unlimited, Inc./Louise Murray/Getty Images; 49bmr: Keith Ellenbogen/Blue Reef; 49br: Jason Isley/Scubazoo; 50, 51tl: Keith Ellenbogen/Blue Reef; 51tc, 51bl, 51bc, 51br: iStockphoto; 51tr: Scubazoo; 51bmr: Stephen Frink/Science Faction/Corbis; 52–53: Alain Machet/Alamy; 54–55: Yi Lu/Corbis; 54tr, 54tmr, 54tmr, 54bc: iStockphoto; 54tml: Peter Johnson/Corbis; 54tmcl: Bodil Bluhm, University of Alaska Fairbanks, with NOAA funding; 54tmr: D.R. Schrichte/SeaPics; 54bml: Saul Gonor/SeaPics.com; 54cmr: J. Gutt, AWI/MARUM, University of Bremen, Germany; 54bl: Ben Cranke/Getty Images; 54br: Paul Oomen/Getty Images; 55tr: Paul Souders/Corbis; 55tmc: Doug Allan/Getty Images; 55bl: Flip Nicklin/Getty Images; 55bcr, 55bmr, 55b: iStockphoto; 55bc: Gerald Kooyman/Corbis; 56–57: World Travel Collection/Alamy; 58–59: Jim Richardson/National Geographic/Corbis; 58bl: Wolfgang Kaehler/Corbis; 58tcr, 58tr, 58tmcr, 58tmr, 58bmcr, 58br: iStockphoto; 59tcr, 59tr, 59tml, 59tmc, 59bml, 59bmc, 59bl, 59bc, 59br: iStockphoto; 59cr: Wayne Lynch/All Canada Photos/Corbis; 60–61: Georgette Douwma/Getty Images; 60bl: Reinhard Dirscherl/SeaPics; 60tcr: Brandon Cole Marine Photography/Alamy; 60tr, 60bmcr: iStockphoto; 60tmcr, 60tmr: Espen Rekdal/SeaPics; 60bmr: Shutterstock; 60br: Masa Ushioda/SeaPics; 61tl: Jason Isley/Scubazoo/Science Faction/Corbis; 61tr: Blickwinkel/Alamy; 61tml: Visuals Unlimited/Corbis; 61tmc, 61bml, 61bmc, 61bl, 61bcl, 61bcr, 61br: iStockphoto; 61tmr: Specialist Stock/Corbis; 61bmr: Stuart Westmorland/Corbis; 63br: Colin Keates/Dorling Kindersley, Courtesy of the Natural History Museum, London; 64–65: DLILLC/Corbis; 66tl: Visuals Unlimited/Corbis; 66cl: DK Limited/Corbis; 68tcl: NOAA; 68bml: Dante Fenolio/Photo Researchers; 68bl: NOAA; 68tr, 68br: David Shale/Nature Picture Library; 69tml: Norbert Wu/Science Faction/Corbis; 69tr: Visual&Written/Newscom; 69bl: Dave Forcucci/SeaPics.com; 69bc: David Shale/Nature Picture Library; 69br: Dante Fenolio/Photo Researchers; 70l: Associated Press; 70c: Lebrecht Music and Arts Photo Library/Alamy; 70r: Bettmann/Corbis; 72–73: Frans Lanting/Corbis; 72cl: Roman/Getty; 73tl, 73tmr, 73bmr: iStockphoto; 73tr: Bloomberg via Getty Images; 73br: Michael Schmeling/Alamy; 74–75: Guilain Grenier/Oracle Racing; 74tml: iStockphoto; 74bml: Miguel Villagran/dpa/Corbis; 75tr: Associated Press; 75br: Getty Images; 76–77: Bettmann/Corbis; 77cr: Imagno/Getty Images; 78tr: JAMSTEC; 80bl: Colin Keates/Getty Images; 81bl, 81bc, 81br: iStockphoto; 82–83: Abner Kingman/Aurora; 84–85: Shutterstock; 84–85 background: Mike Agliolo/Corbis; 84tl, 84bl: Shutterstock; 84tmcr: Lebrecht Music & Arts/Corbis; 84bmcl: Mary Evans Picture Library; 84br: PoodlesRock/Corbis; 85tl: Lebrecht Music & Arts/Corbis; 85tr: Shutterstock; 85ml: Lebrecht Music and Arts Photo Library/Alamy; 85bcr: The Print Collector/Corbis; 85br: Getty Images; 86–87: Rex Features; 86tml: Shutterstock; 86tr: iStockphoto; 87tl: Rex Features; 87tc: Hulton Archive/Getty Images; 87tr: Damien Simonis/Getty Images; 87tmr, 87bmcr: Shutterstock; 87bmr: Nir Elias/Reuters/Corbis; 88–89: The Bridgeman Art Library; 90–91: Associated Press; 90tl: Shutterstock; 91tl, 91tc, 91tr: Photo Researchers; 92tl, 92bml, 92bl, 92bc, 92br: Mary Evans Picture Library; 92tml: Ralph White/Corbis; 92tr: Superstock; 93tl, 93tr, 93b: Ralph White/Corbis; 94l, 94c: iStockphoto; 94r: Doc White/SeaPics; 96–97: Bloomberg/Getty Images; 96bl: iStockphoto; 96tmr: Michael Schmeling/Alamy; 97tl, 97tc, 97tr: iStockphoto; 98–99: Tony Craddock/Tim Vernon, LTH NHS Trust/Photo Researchers; 98bmcl: Shutterstock; 99tr, 99tmr, 99mr, 99bmr, 99br: iStockphoto; 100–101: Doc White/SeaPics; 100tl: iStockphoto; 100bl: Jason Isley/Scubazoo/Science Faction/Corbis; 101tl, 101tr, 101tmr: iStockphoto; 101tml, 101br: Doc White/SeaPics.com; 101bml: Andrew J. Martinez/SeaPics.com; 101bmr: Howard Hall/SeaPics.com, Inc.; 101bl: Doug Perrine/SeaPics; 102tl,102cl: Daniel Costa; 102br: Bodil Bluhm, University of Alaska Fairbanks/NOAA; 102–103: NOAA; 103tr: Associated Press; 103tmcl: Yoshihiro Fujiwara/JAMSTEC; 103tmcr: Kevin Raskoff, Ph.D.; 103bml: Yoshihiro Fujiwara/JAMSTEC; 103bmcr: James Davis Reimer, Ph.D.; 103b: Larry Madin/Woods Hole Oceanographic Institution; 104–105: Keith Ellenbogen/Blue Reef; 106tr, 106br: iStockphoto; 106tmcl, 106tmcr, 106tmr, 106bmcl, 106bmcr, 106bmr: Shutterstock; 106bl: David Fleetham/Alamy; 107tl, 107tc, 107tr, 107tml, 107tmc, 107bml, 107bmc, 107bmr: Shutterstock; 107tmr: Kevin Schafer/Corbis; 107bl, 107bc: iStockphoto; 107br: Paul Nicklen/Getty Images.

The credits for the images on pages 4–5 can be found on pages 52–53, 62–63, 84–85, and 100–101.

ARTWORK

12l: Andrew Kerr/Dotnamestudios; 12r: Kevin Tildsley/Planetary Visions; 16–17: Andrew Kerr/Dotnamestudios; 16bl, 16bcl, 16bcr, br: Kevin Tildsley/Planetary Visions; 18–19, 20–21c: Kevin Tildsley/Planetary Visions; 78–79c, 80–81c: Tim Loughead/Precision Illustration.

COVER

Front cover: background: Carson Ganci/Design Pics/Corbis, foreground: Reinhard Dirscherl/Visuals Unlimited/Corbis; Back cover: tr: Warren Bolster/Getty Images; cr: Doug Perrine/Nature Picture Library; bl: Manaemedia/Dreamstime.com.

Credits and acknowledgment